# PRAISE FOR *BUSINESS SOS!* & RICH SIERRA, ESQ.

Being in business for over twenty years, you think you have it all figured out. This book is a great reminder that we need a great expert attorney in our corner and more importantly, we need to call on them more. One simple mistake could be detrimental to your success. I am so thankful for this book; it's a reminder to stay in your lane and to never assume you understand the legal jargon. The cost of navigating legal matters on your own will be far less than getting a business attorney involved from the beginning. Having the peace of mind that you are entering into an arrangement and the risk it mitigates could truly be priceless. Can you afford not to?

**Allison Duine**
*President, Intersection Online, Inc.*

*Business SOS!* is an excellent technical-legal guide written in easy-to-understand language and perfect for aspiring and current entrepreneurs of any level. Great job Rich!

**Joaquín M. Nieves**
*President, MultiPak Postal Service*

As entrepreneurs, we are so quick and excited to get a deal done. This book has given us great practical knowledge we can actually understand and apply to our business. This book is a must read for any business owner.

When we first read this book, we had so many assumptions about how we should work with our attorney. *Business SOS!* made it easy for us to understand that having a lawyer who has your back can really save you from a bad decision when making a deal.

**Caroline Castille and Mike Sierra**
*Founders, Clickable Impact*

# BUSINESS SOS!

Rich Sierra, Esq.

# BUSINESS SOS!

Eight Common Legal Mistakes
Business Owners Make and
How to Avoid Them

 | Books

Published by Advantage, Charleston, South Carolina.
Member of Advantage Media.

ADVANTAGE is a registered trademark, and the Advantage colophon is a trademark of Advantage Media Group, Inc.

Printed in the United States of America.

10 9 8 7 6 5 4 3 2 1

ISBN: 978-1-64225-571-3 (Hardcover)
ISBN: 978-1-64225-576-8 (Paperback)
ISBN: 978-1-64225-575-1 (eBook)

LCCN: 2022919297

Cover photography by Graciela Laurent Photography.
Cover design by Matthew Morse.
Layout design by David Taylor.

This publication is designed to provide accurate and authoritative information in regard to the subject matter covered. It is sold with the understanding that the publisher is not engaged in rendering legal, accounting, or other professional services. If legal advice or other expert assistance is required, the services of a competent professional person should be sought.

Advantage Media helps busy entrepreneurs, CEOs, and leaders write and publish a book to grow their business and become the authority in their field. Advantage authors comprise an exclusive community of industry professionals, idea-makers, and thought leaders. Do you have a book idea or manuscript for consideration? We would love to hear from you at **AdvantageMedia.com**.

*I'd like to dedicate this book to the smartest businesswoman
I've ever known, my mother, Rosa. For over thirty years she
owned a small beauty shop named Rose Coiffure, in Levittown,
Puerto Rico, and was the only source of income to support our
family and put me through college. It is through her that I got
the inspiration to venture into my own business. She is my best
friend, confidant, and business advisor.*

*Gracias, Mami! Te Quiero Mucho!*

*Ricky*

# CONTENTS

# FOREWORD

## By Philip Fairley

I was wrong.

I have been wrong before. I believe that as a business owner, if you have achieved any level of success, you have been wrong too. I also believe that there are vastly different levels of wrong in business.

Almost twenty-five years ago when I started my first tech firm, I was given some sage advice: "If you want to succeed, you need a top-notch business attorney, an accountant and then a mentor." Of course, I didn't take the advice. Just like I didn't take the advice of my friends to not start a technology company during the dotcom bubble burst of 2000. I was a smart new business owner! An entrepreneur. The rising star that would be able to navigate any situation thrown my way! I was the innovator. I was going to do it better than anyone that had come before. Or at the very least as *well* as the best.

Some lessons you can't be told. You just hope the deficiencies in your learning are more building blocks than terminal events.

I have known Rich Sierra in different environments, but always as someone that shares a similar passion: helping entrepreneurs. The risk takers. Rich has successfully piloted the business owners' journey several times in his life: initially by founding, managing, growing and selling a high-tech healthcare company at a time when high-tech was dialup internet. His drive then inspired him to create the Florida Small Business Legal Center where he dedicates his time to helping owners navigate the legalities of running a business. In my opinion, this is one of the most overlooked parts of being an owner... until it *can't* be overlooked.

When I was approached to read a prepublished copy of his manuscript, he described it as a business book inspired by his clients. So of course, I was excited. He has some really interesting clients and does some really interesting and valuable legal work for them. When I picked it up just to glance over the table of contents, I ended up reading the whole book front to back. Then after reading the first chapter, I started taking notes. Some new things I needed to address at Rainmaker. And then some old things, that just burned. They burned because they were painful lessons that I had to learn the hard way. The hands-on way. The stubborn way. The expensive way.

About two years into my first technology business, my hard work was really starting to pay off. I was finally able to land my first large client—a mid-market logistics company a little outside of Chicago. So being the innovator that I was, I just grabbed a free 'internet-influenced' contract I found on a random website. Sounded official enough. So, I thought, *let me use this great new contract I have for the new software consultant I needed to hire for the project.*

I discovered that a homebrewed contract can cost you $50,000, a critical client, an engineer, thirteen months of court continuances, one failed round of arbitration, and a hotly negotiated settlement on the morning of the trial. For ten cents on the dollar. At the end of the day, it was far from free.

The genius of this legal manual is that it isn't a legal manual. It's a practical guide to specific areas of the law you must know. The lessons apply across all business types, formations, industries and sizes.

Being a business owner that has the courage to go after their dreams and make a positive impact in their world must also know how to protect that dream. That's what this book will help you do. Understand that a handshake and 'common sense' won't defend the legacy you are creating.

I am proud of owning one of the largest legal marketing firms, The Rainmaker Institute, and humbled by our talented staff. Even though we have over twenty attorneys on payroll, this books still motivated me to create a list of items we are going to address in our next weekly leadership meeting.

I am excited that you have picked up this book. If you read it and act on the practical advice Rich Sierra lays out, it will save you from potentially fatal situations that too many of us stubborn business owners learn the hard way.

*Philip Fairley is the President and Chief Innovation Officer of The Rainmaker Institute (therainmakerinstitute.com) and runs the first and only practical bootcamp for attorneys on how to grow their law firm into a business: Rainmaker Retreats (rainmakerretreats.com)*

# INTRODUCTION

Hiring an attorney to handle a business dispute can be stressful. Yet it's important to do so. As a business owner, you're already distracted by the legal matter's potential impact on your livelihood. And if you're like many business owners, you may have already looked for solutions online or asked a friend or relative to help you. Once you've exhausted these self-help options, though, you may feel overwhelmed and confused. Or maybe you're concerned about handling such a serious matter yourself. So you begin searching for legal counsel, asking around for referrals and reviewing lawyers' websites. You may narrow your selection to two or three law firms and start scheduling meetings.

While such diligence is necessary and commendable, you may continue to feel anxious. The time you're spending is keeping you away from your business, and you may be concerned that consulting a professional will cost more time and more money than you can afford.

Alternatively, perhaps you're not yet in business, not facing a lawsuit, but afraid that should you go into business, you may be at risk of one at some future point. You might also fear that you will open yourself up to a variety of other business-related issues. You might, for example, have a great idea for a business but know that you have little or no experience running one. Your business model might be based on unrealistic expectations, such as that customers pay on time. You might also be aware that you have no real understanding of how receivables are collected, have no idea what cash-flow management is about, have trouble remembering what terms like working capital mean, and find the contractual agreements you're faced with signing difficult to understand. Yet, excited about being your own boss, you may ignore these concerns, figuring you'll work it all out as you go. After all, you tell yourself, hiring a lawyer might break your already cash-strapped budget, and anyway, the last thing you want is for some attorney to burst your bubble.

*If any of this rings true for you, or if you find yourself in any of these situations, this book is for you.* It will show you how an initial consultation with a business attorney can help you get out of legal problems, limit the likelihood that legal or any other business-related issues will occur, and show you how the value of an initial consultation far outweighs its cost and can even save you money. A business attorney can be your lifeline when you are faced with a legal issue in your business, which you are likely to face at some point.

Why am I qualified to offer you the advice in this book? Well, I'm not only an attorney—I'm a business owner myself. During the last twenty-five-plus years, I've run two successful businesses: the first was HealthcareRecruitment.com, a website that provided job postings for the healthcare industry, and the second is my own law firm, Florida Small Business Legal Center. Also, *I am passionate about small business*! I am fascinated by the organic nature of small business, and developing an idea to see it turn into a money-making venture is an exciting ride, not only one that have I had the opportunity to enjoy myself but also one that I enjoy taking with my clients. I learn as much from my clients' experiences as my clients learn from my professional advice.

In my practice, I take every opportunity to learn about my clients' businesses and how they came to establish them. Understanding my clients' businesses helps me develop effective legal strategies for them. During my eighteen years as a business lawyer, I have assisted thousands of clients, ranging from restaurant, franchise, and shoe store owners to software developers, manufacturing companies, martial arts schools, auto repair shops, entertainers, and many other types of small business owners.

The first step in this process is an initial consultation. What is an initial consultation? If the matter involves a lawsuit, an initial consultation involves evaluating at least the following seven factors, all of which help to determine whether there is a potential case, and if so, how strong it is:

*Liability:* Who is responsible for the harm to your business, and can you establish this by holding the other party accountable under one or more legal theories, such as breach of contract, unfair competition, or fraud?

*Damages:* "Damages" is a legal term regarding harm suffered by another party's wrongful conduct. In most business cases, damages are measured in terms of financial loss, as opposed to physical injury or emotional distress.

*Who is the potential defendant?* This part of an evaluation concerns identifying who the potential defendant is and whether they have assets or insurance to satisfy a judgment.

*Strength of evidence:* Strength of evidence relates to whether you have documentation to support your case.

*Jury selection and presentation of evidence:* Let's face it, most business disputes are resolved prior to reaching the trial stage; however, it is important to evaluate the likelihood that a jury will believe your side of the story, as well as how credible the jury is likely to find any witnesses you may have.

*Availability of a favorable forum:* Considerations regarding this part of the evaluation of your case involve assessing whether your contract mandates arbitration or, if the case goes to court, which court governs the matter at hand, which local rules may apply, and whether the attitudes of prospective judges and jurors in those locales are likely to be receptive to your claims.

*Client mindset/objectives:* An initial consultation also includes an evaluation of your goals in resolving the dispute. These might include fair compensation for harm suffered, public validation, and/ or punishing the defendant.

As I said, the variety of business owners I've had the privilege to assist has taught and continues to teach me a great deal. For example, one of the most important lessons I've learned about practicing law is that there's more than one "right way" of doing things. I therefore take a customized approach to clients' legal problems and business concerns, basing my advice on their individual goals, time constraints, and budget limitations. After all, as a business owner myself, I understand that independence and individuality are at the core of my fellow business owners' values. Clients often need unique solutions, require immediate attention, and frequently have limited financial resources.

Unfortunately, I often find the issues clients face could have been avoided if they'd sought legal advice prior to entering the business transaction. Don't get me wrong; it's very common to enter into contracts and business transactions without the advice of an attorney. However, as previously noted, many business owners rely on the advice of a friend, neighbor, or family member instead of consulting a professional. Such people usually have very good intentions but, due to lack of expertise, sometimes provide the wrong legal advice, perhaps making the situation even worse.

Why, you may ask, do business owners, people who are otherwise responsible and sensible in their business affairs, do this? Frequently, when I ask a client why they didn't hire a lawyer prior to entering into a business transaction, the reply is, "To save money in legal fees." This answer is so prevalent it's the first of the mistakes I discuss in this book. Other often cited reasons include "I thought I understood the contract," "My brother helped me," and so on and so forth.

Such answers, frankly, do not make sense. As a new business owner, you're about to invest thousands of dollars in opening a new business, entering into a multiyear lease, using personal savings and credit to finance the venture, signing contracts with vendors, developing a brand, spending thousands in advertising and marketing, and devoting countless hours to the endeavor *before you so much as achieve your first sale.* Yet you're not willing to spend a few hundred dollars for a consultation with an attorney to advise you about a legal problem or to help you steer clear of potential legal land mines or other business challenges?

If that's your thinking, unfortunately, it's simply unrealistic. Like most things in life, no business venture can be undertaken without encountering risks and problems. You may never face legal issues in your business (although it's unlikely), but why risk being unprotected if you do, especially when affordable legal help to limit the possibility of litigation and/or enable its speedy resolution is available?

Another common reply to this question is "I was afraid a lawyer would talk me out of it." Please don't be concerned about this. This worry, in fact, only shows that you understand it would be prudent to do so. Talking clients out of going into business is not an attorney's role. The role of a business lawyer is first, to identify legal issues affecting your business, and second, to offer legal options available to address such issues. In fact, a consultation with an attorney can *save* you thousands of dollars (and headaches) later on, as you grow your business.

The goals of this book, therefore, are to share some of the insights and observations I have arrived at after consultations with thousands of business owners, to help you avoid some of the common mistakes I've seen them make, and to reveal some of the mistakes that I myself have made (because, yes, as a small business owner, I've learned some lessons the hard way, and I hope to spare you my own trials and tribulations). Consequently, this book is not a how-to guide or a compilation of forms; instead, it discusses the types of mistakes I commonly either see clients making, counsel them about preventing, or attempt to fix after they have already made them. I hope that in addition to offering a broad scope of examples of the types of legal issues that can arise in business and the potential ways consultation with an attorney can resolve or help prevent them, this book will also illustrate situations in which you should call an attorney *before* a problem arises or before an issue escalates and costs ten times more than necessary. One more thing, nothing in this book constitutes legal advice regarding your particular situation. The examples provided are hypotheticals and should not be construed as pertaining to a specific set of circumstances. If you have a legal problem, I recommend you seek the advice of an attorney.

**BUSINESS TAKES HARD WORK, PASSION, THOUGHT, PLANNING, DISCIPLINE, CREATIVITY, CONTINUED EVALUATION, AND ADJUSTMENTS ALONG THE WAY.**

*Being in business for yourself is tough. Things will go wrong, and you need to be prepared. Business takes hard work, passion, thought, planning, discipline, creativity, continued evaluation, and adjustments along the way.* Chances are that if you have a successful business now, you've probably already experienced a few issues or even failures, and perhaps the business you're in right now was not the one you first envisioned. If so, you're not alone. As I said, as a business owner, I too have had my share of such challenges. Yet despite all the difficult times, disappointments, wild rides, long nights, uncertainty, and tears, I would not trade the thrill of business ownership for anything. The sense of freedom and independence it affords is truly unmeasurable. The confidence to know that you are able to make things happen regardless of how the economy is doing is true freedom, and the good news is that there are myriad resources available to help you start your own business and show you how to make it successful.

I hope you will find that this book is one of them. Thank you for taking the time to read it. I welcome your feedback at Rich@RichSierra.com.

Sincerely,

***Rich Sierra, Esq.***
CEO and Founder
Florida Small Business Legal Center
https://FloridaSmallBusinessLegalCenter.com
https://www.linkedin.com/in/richard-sierra-4501054/
https://richsierra.com/

## MISTAKE 1

# NOT HIRING A LAWYER TO SAVE MONEY

As business owners, we are self-sufficient by nature. Natural problem solvers, we believe in do-it-ourselves solutions. We are also often either short on financial resources, or what money we do have is allocated for business expenses. Since information about common legal questions is available to us right from our mobile devices, it may seem both straightforward and inexpensive to find answers to such questions online. However, it is rarely, if ever, a good idea to rely solely on the web when you're looking for answers to legal problems. And often, trying to save money on initial consultation fees usually ends up costing you more cash, time, and peace of mind than necessary.

Take, for example, the case of a client of mine who recently contacted me regarding being sued for breach of contract. The client, a corporate entity, had defaulted on a payment and so received a judgment requesting monies owed. However, instead of consulting an attorney to help him respond to the court order, he ignored it repeatedly. As a result, he subsequently received a writ of attachment. The writ ordered that he be arrested unless he complied with the court's order to supply the financial information requested. Yes, simply because he'd avoided consulting a professional right away, he suddenly found what had started as a fairly simple legal matter had escalated to a serious situation.

This client now stood to lose much time and money as well as to suffer damage to his reputation. However, his legal issue was so complicated by the time he finally contacted me that it was necessary to do much more than respond to a simple court order. Instead, I had to trace the series of events leading up to the point at which he had received the writ of attachment, as well as collect bank statements, tax returns, and other financial documents for presentation to the court. My services, therefore, ended up costing him much more time and money, not to mention sleepless nights, than necessary.

Not every business owner, of course, ignores court orders while they search online for do-it-yourself legal solutions. Nor are the consequences of every business owner's attempt to handle legal challenges so dire. This is just one of the more dramatic examples I've encountered. But this illustration serves to show how trying to do it yourself can ultimately make a legal situation more complex and much more costly.

Here are a few more of the many reasons why contacting an attorney is usually the best choice:

# 1. Your legal problem is unique and deserves a tailored legal evaluation.

The successful resolution of legal issues depends on detailed analysis of your specific situation, including the circumstances that brought you to being involved in a legal action in the first place. This is because while it may seem from articles or blogs you read online that there's a one-size-fits-all way to deal with the particular legal challenge you face, the reality is that legal actions don't arise overnight. Instead, they are the result of an accumulation of facts and conditions related to that legal challenge—and those circumstances are always unique.

# 2. It is not possible to replace the advice you would receive from a qualified professional about your legal issue from an article or a blog.

Articles and blogs are simply too generic to apply more than generally to your nuanced and specific situation. They can't be considered legal advice, and more likely than not, if you rely and act on this information, it will cost you more later to hire an attorney to attempt to fix the mistake.

# 3. "Consulting" with a friend, family member, neighbor, or relative who isn't a legal professional can end badly.

The old adage "Never do business with a friend" is a truism for a reason and applies also to consulting those unqualified to give legal advice. Sometimes, for instance, relying on a friend or other nonlegal professional can result in anything from serious oversights in terms of legal analysis to errors such as failure to observe procedural rules and/or missing deadlines, all of which can devastate your case.

# 4. Business law is very technical, and some mistakes are irreversible.

Business law regards any type of legal matter that involves a business. The practice of business law involves a myriad of types of contracts and includes many considerations. Consequently, navigating its complexities is, well, complex, and attempting to do so can result in irreversible mistakes. Sometimes, for example, business owners who attempt it actually end up waiving options or defenses that would have solved their issue, simply because they either didn't understand them, overlooked them, or pursued some unsuccessful or less successful alternative line of defense.

# 5. Purchasing a business involves many considerations you either may not be aware of or may not know how to handle.

When entering into an asset-purchase agreement, for example, it's important to be sure the business has (among many other items to consider) no outstanding debts. Many debts are not on the public record, so obtaining the seller's disclosures as to bank accounts, a list of all contracts, and whether there are any liens on the business is essential. Any unpaid liabilities, such as payroll taxes, must also be disclosed and paid prior to closing your purchase, or you could be faced with paying them yourself. If, for instance, a business uses independent contractors versus employees, and therefore hasn't included withholdings, when the business is sold, those independent contractors may demand overtime payment from the new owner. An attorney can help you identify such red flags, making you aware that you need to ask more questions and how to answer them.

# 6. Price should not be the determining factor when hiring an attorney.

Instead of making price your sole criterion, consider the following questions:

### What is the cost of the legal problem if I do nothing?

Obviously, if you're being sued for a particular amount, you know how much you will owe if you lose your case. However, sometimes additional, unforeseen costs can arise, such as in the aforementioned case of the client who postponed seeking legal counsel until his situation was so complex he couldn't avoid doing so. As noted, by then, the cost of handling the legal problem had increased considerably.

## What is the cost if I handle a legal transaction myself?

One type of cost that commonly occurs when small business owners attempt to handle the legal aspects of business transactions, such as setting up or selling businesses by themselves, is the cost of not doing the proper due diligence on both sides. People encounter this all the time. Either they're friends with someone they're going into business with or friends with the seller of the business they want to buy. And because they know each other, they are often laid back with respect to the due diligence that needs to be done by both parties in the process of purchase and sale. If, for example, a would-be small business owner decides to buy a business from a friend, he or she may not feel it necessary to ensure that the lease is assignable—in other words, that the landlord is willing to sign over the remaining portion of the lease agreement.

Another type of cost, of course, is the time that handling a legal problem yourself takes away from your business, time that could be better spent making money and growing your business.

## Even if I don't yet have a legal challenge, what costs might I incur down the road if I try to set up a business without consulting an attorney?

There are many DIY legal forms online, making it tempting to set up a business without legal counsel. However, such forms are often so basic they may not be adequate to your unique business needs, which may lead to costly legal problems in future. For example, they might not pertain to the particular jurisdiction in which your business is established, or they might be out of date, omit provisions essential to your business type, or fail to account for situations you may find yourself facing.

## What is the cost of a one-hour initial consultation with an attorney who has experience handling this issue and can advise me on my possible legal options?

The cost of an initial consultation with an attorney is generally just a few hundred dollars, while the cost of dealing with legal issues is usually in the thousands or hundreds of thousands, not to mention the time it will cost you away from your business. Unfortunately, though, some business owners make $100,000 mistakes for attempting to save those few hundred dollars. It's just not worth the risk.

I can list more such reasons to consult an attorney prior to going into business or deciding to handle a legal matter yourself, but you get the point. Many legal issues could be prevented if the business owners involved simply consulted an attorney at the first sign of a legal challenge or, better yet, prior to opening their doors.

> **MANY LEGAL ISSUES COULD BE PREVENTED IF THE BUSINESS OWNERS INVOLVED SIMPLY CONSULTED AN ATTORNEY AT THE FIRST SIGN OF A LEGAL CHALLENGE.**

# Your First Meeting with a Business Lawyer

I receive hundreds of calls every month from people facing legal disputes who have researched their situations online yet still have questions about how to resolve them. Often, however, they're hesitant to schedule a consultation, perhaps because they don't know what to expect, don't understand the value a consultation offers, or perhaps even because they're offended to learn there's a fee involved.

Let's look at each of these concerns individually.

In terms of what to expect from an initial consultation, there are several typical components. Below, for example, are some common topics you might discuss with your attorney during that first meeting:

- The circumstances that led you to schedule the appointment

- The option(s) presented by the attorney to address the legal issue

- Your goals and expectations, and questions as to whether they are attainable

- Fees and cost for services, as well as the billing process

- How long it will take for the legal matter to conclude

- The attorney's concerns about the case (what is not in your favor)

- The possibility for an early mediation to discuss settlement

- How often you will receive updates on the case

- Best- and worst-case scenarios

- Likely scenarios based on the attorney's experience handling similar cases

Additionally, your attorney may discuss your situation from both legal and business perspectives. Many of the initial consultations I conduct, for example, focus mainly on the feasibility of my clients' business ventures. This aspect of an initial consultation is, in fact, a significant value to my clients, as it helps them decide whether the business decision they're considering making is the right one. While, again, it's in no way my role to talk anyone out of his or her ideas, what I can do is to ask some very basic questions about financing, about how revenue's going to be generated, and about how expenses will be met. I ask these questions not only to make sure clients are grounded in the fundamentals of any business venture but because lack of attention to any of these areas can lead to legal issues. In this way, I often act as much as a business consultant as an attorney.

One of the misconceptions I often hear about initial consultations, or about consulting attorneys in general, is that they're mainly useful for drafting legal documents or for confirming that legal documents are in fact "legal." These are just some, however, of the many services attorneys offer. Because while drafting and examining legal documents are indeed useful services, they are not necessarily the most important. Legal documents are valid and legally binding 99 percent of the time. Therefore, any issue that arises with them does not usually concern their legality. The issue instead is often whether the document is written in such a way that it's in your best interests and truly reflects what you agreed to in the transaction. There's a big distinction between something being "legal" and something being in your "best interests," and just because it's a legal document does not mean that the legal transaction you're considering entering into is advantageous for you. You can enter into a perfectly well-written contract that will cancel out your finances, making doing so a really bad business decision.

That's why it's important to go into not only the legality of a document but also why the document was created, what you want out of the deal, and what your agenda is over the long term. Such in-depth questions go a long way to helping you decide whether the document you have in hand is one you want to sign, or whether it details the kind of agreement you want to go into, and the answers help to protect you against any potential legal challenges going forward.

# Types of Legal Challenges

If you aren't yet convinced that consulting with an attorney is more prudent and cost effective than forging ahead alone, consider the following types of legal situations, situations categorized under various areas of business law, that small business owners frequently encounter:

## Arbitration

- A business owner receives a notice of arbitration from the American Arbitration Association and needs representation at the arbitration hearing

## Breach of Contract

- A business partner is sued by another partner for breach of contract

- A small business is served with a lawsuit by a vendor for breach of contract

## Buying / Selling a Business

- A business owner would like to purchase a franchise and needs assistance reviewing the franchise disclosure document and franchise agreement

- A business owner would like to purchase real estate, a property for the business

- A business owner would like to expand his or her operation and needs legal advice about the best options for expansion

## Commercial Lease Agreements

- A small business owner would like to have a lease agreement reviewed and negotiated

- A business was shut down due to a government mandate; the owner has questions on whether he still needs to pay his commercial lease while he is closed

## Drafting/Reviewing of Documents

- A small business owner needs assistance in developing new contracts for her company

- Shareholders of a privately held corporation would like to add another shareholder and need a new shareholder agreement drafted

- A business owner would like to purchase another business and needs an asset-purchase agreement drafted

- A business owner would like to sell her business and needs assistance in drafting a stock purchase agreement

- A small business owner needs assistance in drafting an employment agreement for her employees

- A small business owner needs assistance in drafting an independent contractor agreement for her employees

- Business owners who are partners in a business would like assistance drafting a buy-sell agreement

- A business owner of an LLC needs to draft an operating agreement

- A business owner would like to enter into a joint venture with another business and needs a joint venture agreement drafted

- A small business owner is applying for SBA loans and needs assistance reviewing the loan agreement

## Due Diligence

- A business owner would like to join as a new member of an LLC and needs assistance in conducting the due diligence review and the purchase agreement to join as a new member

## Franchising

- The owner of a restaurant business would like to franchise his restaurant and take it nationwide

- A franchisee is sued by the franchisor for breach of the franchise agreement

## Licensing

- A business owner would like to develop a licensing agreement to license his logo and intellectual property to other business owners

## Litigation

- A business owner in a litigation case needs representation at the mediation conference

- A business is sued by a client for negligence, for damages she allegedly suffered while on the business premises

- A business owner is sued for an alleged COVID-19 infection and needs representation

- A business owner discovers that a former employee stole confidential business information and trade secrets from the company and would like to know what to do

- A tenant of a commercial property is sued by the landlord for eviction and back rent

- A business owner receives a subpoena for a deposition and needs representation

- A business owner is being sued for alleged violation of a non-compete agreement

- A business owner is sued for alleged violations of the Florida Trade Secrets Act and the Florida Deceptive and Unfair Trade Practices Act

- A business owner receives a subpoena for documents and needs assistance on how to respond

- A business owner was not paid by a client and needs assistance collecting on the amount due

## Partnership Disputes

- A business owner's partner shuts her out of the business by removing her name from the organization's bank accounts, and she needs immediate representation

- A business owner discovers that his partner is stealing funds from the company

- A business owner finds out that her partner opened a competing company and is diverting clients to the new company

- A partner in a small business needs legal assistance on what to do when the partner abandons the business

- A business owner needs representation on negotiating a settlement agreement and buyout with his partner

- A business owner would like to expand his operation and needs legal advice about the best options for expansion

- A business owner is sued by a former partner for breach of fiduciary duty and would like to file a counterclaim

- A business owner needs to sue her partner for breach of the partnership agreement

## Trademarks

- A small business owner needs assistance in registering a trademark

- A small business owner is sued for trademark infringement

- A business owner finds out that a competitor is using his trademark, and it is creating confusion with potential customers

Don't make a costly mistake just to save a few hundred on an initial consultation. If worrying about legal problems (or even the potential for such problems) keeps you awake at night, consider consulting a professional. I promise you'll sleep better, resolve or prevent legal woes, possibly receive other sound business advice, and save more money than you'll spend if you don't.

In the next chapter, we'll discuss the number two mistake small business owners often make: signing a contract before hiring an attorney to review it. As you'll see, while this is an understandable mistake, it often proves to be a serious one.

## MISTAKE 2

# SIGNING A CONTRACT WITHOUT HIRING A LAWYER

It truly surprises me how many people are willing to sign contracts, *contracts that are prepared by attorneys*, before having their own attorney review them and explain their provisions.

Consider this scenario: You and your spouse, partner, or significant other want to start a business selling ice cream. After considerable research and after visiting establishments in your area, you settle for an ABC franchise that you learned from a business broker is for sale near your home. Both of you are excited with the anticipation of owning your own business and claiming your slice of the American dream, so after some discussion, you decide to make an offer to buy it. The business broker sends you a one-page letter of intent, requests a deposit, and lets you know that the funds will be held in *his* account until the deal closes. Your offer is then presented to the owner of the business, and she accepts. Congratulations! You just purchased an ABC franchise. You are happy because you just became a business owner, the seller is happy to sell the franchise, the landlord is happy because her property remains rented, and the broker is happy because he just made a commission. Time to celebrate!

Except that, uh-oh. Now it's time for a reality check. Sorry to kill your buzz. But the story does not end here.

The scenario described above is very common, and I (the attorney) don't usually meet you (the buyer) until something goes wrong, as it did in this situation.

Unfortunately, these buyers did not know when they bought the franchise that the prior owner had not paid employees' payroll taxes. In fact, the owner had not even filed payroll. The owner had instead filed only 1099 forms, as if the employees were independent contractors. Consequently, the buyers subsequently received a letter from the IRS asking for payment of back taxes. To make matters worse, the sellers, as the increasingly dismayed buyers soon discovered, also were in arrears to the state of Florida for failing to pay sales taxes to the Florida Department of Revenue!

Such situations are extremely common, and would-be business owners who become aware of even what may seem minor infractions of this nature should know that, as the saying goes, where there's smoke, there's also usually fire. In other words, often, when a business owner hasn't paid taxes, or bills, or acquired the necessary licensing, or performed necessary renovations, or when the business has been neglected in any other way, it's a red flag. In this case, the owner hadn't paid federal payroll taxes; therefore, it wasn't especially surprising (at least to me) that he was also in arrears of state sales tax.

Under Florida state law, when you buy a business, whoever takes over that business could be held liable for those taxes. In this case, the new owners owed $5,000 in payroll taxes to the IRS and $20,000 in taxes to the Florida Department of Revenue. They therefore attempted to sue the sellers for payment of such amounts, only to find that they had left the country.

Again, this type of situation happens frequently. However, it could easily be avoided simply by meeting with an attorney for a presigning consultation, after which any such potential red flags the attorney identifies could be investigated via a process termed "due diligence."

# Due Diligence

Due diligence as it pertains to the purchase of a business is the process of investigating a business entity, person, or party in preparation for a business or loan transaction. It involves, for instance, reviewing documents, talking to management, visiting the business location, and analyzing risk.

Hiring an attorney to conduct due diligence in any business matter is wise, and when purchasing a new business, you should, at the very least, consult with one to help you understand what to expect—and not only because the previous owners may have neglected to pay debts.

You see, buying a business is different than buying, say, a house. When you buy a house, all kinds of other people and protections are involved, from the bank to the title company to the real estate agent. You therefore have much more security than you do when buying a business. If you're buying a home, the bank won't approve a mortgage if you don't have title insurance, so a neutral, third-party title company does a lien search to see if there's any type of cloud on the title. Meanwhile, the real estate agent educates you on the buying process, overseeing the hiring of an inspector and protecting your deposits and your right to back out of the deal within a certain time frame.

Further, while all these real estate processes are documented on the public record, this is not the case when buying a business.

What people don't realize is this: Even though you can sign a purchase agreement that includes what's called a "warranties and representations" section (attesting that the business does not owe any debts or taxes and the business is free and clear), certain types of debts sometimes are not recorded unless some type of court action has been filed or a lien has been placed against the business.

In addition to unpaid taxes, for example, a seller may owe debts to vendors. Yet if there's no court action or lien on the public record, then unless the seller discloses debt, or unless you get some type of a letter from a government agency informing you of debt, you will not know whether the business is in fact free and clear. In other words, unless you either know specifically what questions to ask and how to obtain the answers, or unless you hire an attorney to conduct due diligence, you could be at risk of being held liable for such debt.

Conducting due diligence will provide access to the tax returns and other business documents as well as ensure those documents have been prepared according to sound accounting principles, are true and complete, and reflect only actual transactions. If you do not do this, you will only be able to find out this information the hard way—such as when the IRS sends a letter demanding payment, or the unpaid vendor puts a lien on your equipment, or when you find out that there's a zoning issue in terms of how the business can operate (as my ever-more-unfortunate clients also discovered after purchasing their "American dream").

New business owners who encounter such situations are really in a predicament. They're starting a business, but the working capital they anticipated using to do so must now be used to pay debts they didn't incur.

The unfortunate reality is this: If you are someone others can identify as having money or credit to purchase a business, you will receive a great deal of attention from those with a vested interest in earning a commission from the transaction. Think about this. Going back, for example, to our original scenario, the now-beleaguered buyers dealt with the landlord, the business broker, the sellers, and the franchisor. Yet all these people acted in their own best interests. Why? Because none of them has a responsibility to act in the buyer's interest. As a new business owner, you need to be aware that it is *your* responsibility to protect your self-interests and your money. The best way to do this is to hire an attorney.

Don't misunderstand me. Most people you'll encounter in your business career are honest professionals. This, however, doesn't change the fact that they don't have the responsibility of protecting you from making a bad financial decision. Also, most of these professionals (such as, for instance, business brokers) already have lawyers working on their behalf, putting you at a disadvantage if you don't. In fact, *one of the main reasons that you need a lawyer before purchasing a new business is to level the playing field.*

The bottom line is, it's just not possible to go into business without facing some legal land mines (unless of course you just never

> **ONE OF THE MAIN REASONS THAT YOU NEED A LAWYER BEFORE PURCHASING A NEW BUSINESS IS TO LEVEL THE PLAYING FIELD.**

open the doors). The challenges you face may be minor or major, but at some point, some legal questions will come up. In fact, a contract itself is a legal question.

# Common Mistakes When Signing Contracts without an Attorney

Let's consider some more possible situations inexperienced would-be business owners get themselves into when signing contracts without first having them reviewed by an attorney:

Often, potential business owners, not wanting to spend the money to consult an attorney, attempt to draft their own contracts and/or download online forms.

This isn't necessarily a mistake. Depending on the transaction and given that many business owners need to preserve capital for start-up costs, their preference for DIY contracts is entirely understandable. Additionally, because contracts don't need to be complex (in essence, a contract is no more than a legally binding agreement between two parties outlining their responsibilities and mutual obligations), drafting your own contract doesn't need to be complicated. Even a note scribbled on a paper napkin can be an enforceable contract, so a self-drafted contract is better than nothing. Similarly, many online forms are quite adequate, and they're usually legally valid and enforceable.

Self-drafted contracts and online forms, however, have limitations. Neither should be viewed as documents that will necessarily serve your interests, either in terms of your particular business needs or over the long term. Self-drafted contracts typically lack components that provide specific protections necessary to your unique situation, and online forms are only generic templates; there's no one-size-fits-all form. Consequently, although each provides a starting point toward legal protection, many lawsuits result from using them, and it's advisable to consult an attorney who can further refine them to address your particular professional requirements and unique business circumstances.

One frequently encountered example of how relying on online forms can go south is demonstrated by the case of a Florida handyman who downloaded a template for a construction contract for home renovation services to cover the terms of work a client had hired him to do. The type of service this unlicensed handyman agreed to perform required a license, so he secured a qualified agent, allowing him to provide the services while he obtained one. He then downloaded the template construction contract and presented it to his client, whereupon both parties signed it. What the handyman did not realize, however, was that the contract stated he was licensed. Consequently, later, when the client decided he wasn't satisfied with his work, he sued for cancellation of the contract, for the return of his deposit, and for fraud.

This matter was eventually resolved amicably. The moral of the story is, though, that if whatever you're hired to do requires state licensure or certification, it's your professional responsibility to know what's required of you before you provide professional services. This is because that responsibility stands regardless of whatever contract you draft or whatever form you download.

There are several common types of contracts business owners and business attorneys deal with. These include release contracts, settlement agreements, buy and sell agreements, and contracts for services—all of which have specific types of pitfalls if they're not handled correctly.

Many independent contractors, for example, such as tradespeople, software developers, and writers, rely on contracts for services to protect themselves in their dealings with clients. It's therefore important to review terms such as the contract's duration, whether the contract is renewable, what happens if it's renewed, how and within what time frame the contract can be terminated, what conditions warrant termination, whether there's a penalty for early termination, and how compensation and any attorney fees will be handled in the case of such termination.

Termination provisions in a contract for services, for instance, might stipulate that the client can terminate the contract only if there's justifiable reason to do so, such as failure to fulfill certain agreed-upon services. Further, they might specify that the independent contractor receive either an hourly fee for time spent prior to termination or liquidated damages, an amount predetermined as fair that the client will pay regardless of whether more or less is owed up to the point at which termination occurred.

Another area it's important to review, not only with regard to contracts for service but with all types of contracts, is the contract's enforceability. In other words, if either party wants to end the contract, what are the vehicles to enforce termination? Do the parties have to go to arbitration or mediation first? And who is responsible for paying attorney fees if they go to court? These are key areas of any contract. Yet many contracts, especially "homegrown" contracts, do not include such provisions.

This is a serious problem for independent contractors in breach of contract claims, because generally it's not possible to seek attorney fees in such claims unless there's a statutory basis for doing so or the contract stipulates entitlement. Independent contractors may therefore be faced with paying the cost of trying to recover their losses by paying the expenses of attempting to enforce the contract.

Enforceability is also often an issue in terms of both the language the contract is written in and geography. If, for instance, you're doing business in the United States, any contract you sign should be in English. One Miami-based business owner I represented discovered this when, after selling his business to a buyer in Argentina for $4 million, that buyer defaulted on the contract. The seller then expected, and was entitled to rely on, the buy and sell agreement's liquidated damages clause to receive compensation of $200,000. However, since the contract was written in Spanish, verifying this term necessitated the expense of hiring a certified translator. Additionally, even given such verification, enforcing the contract posed a challenge, because the buyer was in Argentina. While it's possible to serve a foreign entity for breach of contract, it's neither easy nor inexpensive. And even if an attorney is successful in doing so, collecting damages is often an exercise in futility.

Buy and sell agreements often lead to other types of legal issues too. Let's say, for instance, you're selling a business with an asking price of $100,000, but the would-be buyer has only $70,000. Eager to conclude the deal, you agree to lend the remaining $30,000 to the buyer in the form of a promissory note. You then negotiate and specify in the buy and sell agreement the terms of payment, such as the dates and amounts of periodic payments and the duration of time within which the debt is to be repaid in full.

Simply having said contract in hand, however, does not necessarily ensure you will receive payment. A contract is not a guarantee. In this situation, all you have is a promissory note. Contracts are often only as good as people's commitment to fulfill them. If a party wants to break a contract, they can break it. It's then up to the injured party to enforce it, and, as noted above, that can often prove costly. In this hypothetical scenario, it's likely that you'll spend at least 50 percent of the $30,000 you hope to recover on legal fees to enforce the note.

Rather than rely solely on a buy and sell agreement for legal protection, to reduce potential for exposure, sellers should negotiate as much money up front from buyers as possible—advice they could have obtained for a few hundred dollars during consultation with an attorney.

*No matter what type of contract you're dealing with, clearly defined terms are key.* Duration of contract, how much money is being exchanged, what services are being offered, when monies and services are expected, how termination is handled, and how the contract can be enforced must all be specifically delineated, understood, and agreed to before the contract can be signed. Until this is the case, you don't have a contract. All you have are offers and counteroffers.

Attorneys, of course, cannot force anyone to take one action over another or make you postpone signing a contract until it sufficiently protects your interests. Sometimes clients decide they're willing to take a risk on an unfavorable term in order to go through with the transaction. In such cases, all an attorney can do is educate you as to the potential for such risk to manifest in the form of a legal issue and what it may cost you in the event that it does.

The basic rule of thumb is this: if you don't understand a contract, don't sign it. Even if you think you "pretty much" understand it, if you're not 100 percent sure, have a professional interpret it for you, because contract or not, you have few safeguards when you start a business. The only safeguards are those you create yourself—preferably by hiring an attorney.

In our next chapter, we'll continue to drive this theme home by discussing the risks of attempting to defend yourself in court without a lawyer's professional guidance.

# MISTAKE 3

# DEFENDING A LAWSUIT WITHOUT AN ATTORNEY

Did you know that about 90 percent of small businesses will experience at least one lawsuit, or that between 36 and 53 percent of small businesses are sued every year?

These statistics from the US Small Business Administration (SBA)[1] are of course alarming. Yet equally so is the reality that given the cost of defending yourself against such suits (which, according to the SBA, run anywhere from $3,000 to $150,000),

---

1    Klemm Analysis Group, "Impact of Litigation on Small Business," Small Business Administration Office of Advocacy, no. 265 (October 2015): 1, https://www.sba.gov/sites/default/files/files/rs265tot.pdf.

many small business owners who've been sued decide not to seek legal representation.

As this chapter will illustrate, this is a serious mistake.

Take, for instance, the case of two would-be small business owners who signed a joint venture agreement, then went into the business of selling auto parts together. Initially, each had believed the other trustworthy. After a time, however, one partner began to suspect that the other was stealing some of those parts. So, after conducting an inventory to document his suspicion, he decided to hire an attorney and file a lawsuit. The attorney then filed suit for conversion (deprivation of property), civil theft, and replevin (a court order to return the property).

After being served, though, instead of seeking legal advice, the accused partner simply wrote to the opposing attorney to explain his side of the story. This was a bad idea. The attorney understood the rules of court, the Florida Rules of Civil Procedure, and the relevant statutory law, putting the unrepresented partner being sued at significant disadvantage as he continued filing responses to motions and appearing at hearings without legal counsel. The situation became increasingly problematic, and by the time he contacted me for help, a judgment for replevin had already been issued against him.

Had this client contacted me immediately after being served, this judgment might have been avoided. For one thing, by responding to the suit himself, he'd waived some of the potentially more successful defenses he might have relied on. For another, after I conducted a due diligence, it became clear that the suing partner (plaintiff) hadn't followed certain statutory requirements. Had my client only consulted me earlier, I could have used this information to help defend him.

# Common Mistakes Self-Representing Small Business Owners Sometimes Make

Writing a letter to a judge or opposing attorney to explain the problem from one's own perspective is just one of many common errors small business owners sometimes make when faced with a lawsuit. While it might seem that writing a letter will help plead your case, it will instead likely hurt it. Why? Well, for two reasons: first, it puts you at risk of waiving certain defenses, making you vulnerable to being taken advantage of by opposing counsel; and second, your explanation may include circumstances and events leading up to the lawsuit that could be detrimental to your case.

Unfortunately, I often meet with clients after they've already made this or other such mistakes, making it difficult to undo a "done deal." As the saying goes, "an ounce of prevention is worth a pound of cure."

Sometimes, small business owners, perhaps having watched too many episodes of *Judge Judy* or *The People's Court*, take it upon themselves to self-represent in front of a judge and/or jury. Maybe they feel their story is so convincing, or their innocence so apparent, that they expect doing so will ensure that justice prevails. If so, this is, as they say, "magical thinking," and therefore unrealistic, especially if the case goes to trial. The simple fact is that an unrepresented person who's inexperienced in the law has virtually no chance against an experienced trial attorney and is quite likely to lose the case.

Think of it this way. When your car's brakes give out, do you try to install new ones yourself? Not likely! If you make even one mistake, you put yourself, your passengers, others on the road, and your car itself in significant danger. It's the same when it comes to representing yourself in court. If you try to defend yourself against an experienced attorney, you are at a complete disadvantage. Attorneys know the rules of court, and you don't. Plus, an attorney could make all kinds of allegations about you. For someone who isn't used to such confrontation, this can be very intimidating, making it easy to become flustered and trapped in contradictions.

Small claims court is really the only court in which it's feasible to defend yourself without legal representation. There's more flexibility in small claims court because judges don't expect self-representing parties to know the rules of court (as they do in other divisions of the courts). In Florida, for instance, if the case being brought against you involves less than $8,000, you can try representing yourself. Even so, if your opponent has an attorney, you'll still be at a disadvantage.

Most small business lawsuits that I see involve amounts greater than $8,000 and so are brought in higher courts. The cases I deal with generally concern at least $30,000 and so are tried in circuit court. In Florida, if you're in a corporate entity and your case involves $15,000 or more, you're required to hire an attorney to help you resolve it, and not doing so may involve consequences. For example, the opposing side may move to strike the pleadings or even drop the case because it wasn't filed by an attorney. The court could then grant you time to find an attorney, but if you don't, it could move to dismiss your pleadings or move for default.

Other common mistakes small business owners make when trying to defend themselves in court without representation include trying to negotiate directly with the opposing attorney, attending mediation without an attorney, and even arguing with the judges. Let's look at each of these.

Negotiating directly with an opposing attorney is sort of like fighting a professional boxer. The negotiation is not on a level playing field from the start. For one thing, there's a risk of miscommunication. The legal terminology that attorneys use can be sufficiently confusing to nonattorneys to create misunderstandings. Further, an opposing attorney's professional responsibility is to his or her own client, not to you. Consequently, an opposing attorney may even take advantage of your unrepresented status to attempt to gain information that would help his or her own client. For instance, the attorney may request documents you aren't legally obliged to share, ask you for financial information it's not in your interests to divulge, or withhold information from you that would serve your case. Additionally, sometimes either the self-represented party, the attorney, or both want to resolve things too quickly, which can become problematic. The attorney may suggest a premature settlement, for example, or the self-represented party may volunteer an admission (a statement made by a party to a lawsuit that tends to support the other side's position or diminish their own) that can be used to weaken that party's case.

Anyone who's ever watched a few episodes of *Law and Order* probably knows that attorneys are bound by a rule stipulating that if someone is represented by legal counsel, they can't communicate about the subject of representation with that person unless the counsel consents to doing so. Obviously, that rule was put into effect to protect even represented clients, so by the same token, unrepresented clients should not try to negotiate with opposing attorneys.

Attending mediation without an attorney is another mistake many small business owners make. Likely, they're eager to avoid the cost of legal counsel and the stress of potentially needing to appear in court. Or, possibly, they're unaware that legal representation is advisable during the mediation process. After all, isn't that why mediation exists—so you can settle differences with the help of a mediator alone? Well, the truth is that even when a mediator is involved, you are still better off being represented by an attorney. This is because attorneys, generally speaking, have the negotiation skills, knowledge of the law, and understanding of the significance of the legal threat you face to determine certain questions, such as whether a settlement you're offered is right for you.

Personally, I often recommend early mediation to my clients. A conversation to possibly resolve the dispute is less costly than litigation, and mediation focuses the parties on finding a solution versus fighting in court. Additionally, it allows parties to solve disputes on their own terms versus having somebody else take control of the process on whatever terms the jury wants. But that doesn't mean you don't need legal counsel. Along with the drawbacks of attending mediation without representation, there's also the reality that most of the time, it's attorneys who hire mediators. Mediators are very ethical, and they won't do anything that will unfairly help the opposing side. Nonetheless, they're human beings, and if they've been hired by an opposing attorney with whom they share a professional affinity, they may be predisposed to that attorney's client, which could affect their recommendations.

Finally, issuing verbal threats to an attorney on the opposing side, or becoming confrontational, or appearing in a hearing on Zoom and interrupting the judge (as some upset small business owners have been known to do), never helps your case. This might seem obvious, yet it's a mistake that's easy to make. Small business owners generally know it's never a good idea to act poorly in court, but lawsuits can become emotional, and everyone has a breaking point. Just as clients are human, however, judges and attorneys are also human, and if you do become angry or belligerent in court, it will at best cloud the case and at worst bias it. From that point forward, the case will become an uphill battle for you because what had previously involved only a professional, objective assessment of your situation will now take on a personal aspect. This sometimes leads judges and attorneys to make negative characterizations of clients, which may bear on the facts, especially in situations where the resolution of the dispute rests on one person's word against another's. Respect and civility really go a long way, and lawsuits go far more smoothly, therefore possibly taking less time and money, if you maintain your composure no matter how heated things get.

# Common Types and Costs of Small Business Lawsuits

Some of the most common types of lawsuits filed against small businesses include breach of contract and breach of fiduciary duty. In fact, the SBA study cited previously found that 31.4 percent of lawsuits filed against small business owners are for breach of contract. However, there are also many other types of lawsuits commonly brought against small business owners, such as slip and fall, real property, employment (discrimination and/or workers' compensation), and malpractice suits.

Such suits can be expensive, and according to a study from the National Center for State Courts, the median combined costs of lawsuits of this nature for both parties can easily exceed from $50,000 to above $100,000. The study cites, for instance, the following costs:

- $91,000 for a contract lawsuit, such as a breach of contract suit.

- $54,000 for a premises liability lawsuit, such as a slip and fall suit.

- $66,000 for a real property lawsuit, such as a home defect suit.

- $88,000 for an employment lawsuit, such as a discrimination or workers' compensation suit.

- $122,000 for a malpractice lawsuit, such as a medical malpractice suit.[2]

As noted at the beginning of this chapter, it's natural for small business owners to seek to avoid such costs by attempting to represent themselves in court. Doing so, however, may actually add to the cost, as a capable and experienced attorney can evaluate the likely effectiveness of a variety of legal approaches, efficiently utilize rules and research pertinent precedents, and review your insurance policy to help you ascertain entitlement to potential coverage of costs.

One of my clients, for example, the owner of a gym, received a letter from one of his customers claiming she'd been injured while using the gym's exercise equipment. The customer claimed injury due to equipment malfunction and sued for about $15,000, so the first thing I asked my client was whether he had insurance. Fortunately, the answer was yes, so although the lawsuit had already been filed, we looked at the policy to see if it covered his situation. After confirming it did, we were able to postpone the suit from proceeding until the insurance carrier could take it over. (Helping you decide what type of insurance to take out for your small business is, by the way, another way an attorney can be useful, whether or not you face a lawsuit, as you need coverage specific to your type of business and the potential types of suits that you may face. If, for instance, you're sued for a workers' compensation issue, you'll need workers'

---

2    Tim Parker, "Four Small Business Lawsuit Statistics," Zen Business, December 6, 2021, accessed [September 29, 2022], https://www.zenbusiness.com/blog/4-small-business-lawsuit-statistics/.

compensation insurance; if you're sued with a slip and fall, you'll need general liability coverage.)

Whatever your situation, when faced with a lawsuit, your first thought should never be to try and cut costs by representing yourself. Instead, contact an attorney with expertise in the area you need help with, secure an initial consultation, and during your consultation, ask what ideas the attorney has as to how to resolve the problem. Every attorney has different approaches, but a good attorney will analyze your case and explain options. Select the attorney you feel best understands what your issue is, has a clear idea of the time frame within which you need to resolve it, and can provide you with an estimate of what it may cost to resolve it (or whether your insurance covers it). The attorney should also be able to provide any potential ways to shorten the duration of the case, such as, when potentially beneficial, suggesting mediation or arbitration.

When you're faced with a lawsuit, attempting to represent yourself in court is one of the worst things you can do. There are, of course, also many other mistakes that business owners make that may have pretty awful consequences. In the next chapter, we'll discuss another one: signing a lease agreement without an attorney.

# MISTAKE 4

# SIGNING A COMMERCIAL LEASE AGREEMENT WITHOUT AN ATTORNEY

Imagine that you want to open a sandwich shop. You sign your lease, buy your equipment, and have a sign made, and you're about to move in. But when you go to the city to get your business license, you learn that the space you've just leased is not zoned for a restaurant.

This situation actually happened to one of my clients, and although we eventually succeeded in releasing him from the commercial lease agreement, it took a court battle to do so.

Commercial leases are complex contracts prepared by attorneys to protect their clients, the landlords who own the property. As such, they strongly favor landlords' interests, not those of small business owners trying to lease such property. Further, commercial leases do not protect business owners from liability to the extent that residential leases protect residential tenants. In fact, when it comes to commercial leases, residential landlord/tenant law is practically nonapplicable; when you sign a commercial lease as a tenant, for the most part, you have to abide by whatever rules the landlord has stipulated in that lease.

> **SIGNING A COMMERCIAL LEASE IS ONE OF THE MOST SIGNIFICANT CONTRACTUAL AGREEMENTS THAT BUSINESS OWNERS ENTER INTO.**

*For these and many other reasons, signing a commercial lease is one of the most significant contractual agreements that business owners enter into.* So it's crucial to elicit the help of an attorney who can help to define the rights and responsibilities the lease stipulates, understand terms, negotiate terms, uncover any unclear charges, and ensure you avoid common oversights.

# Defining Rights and Responsibilities

Commercial lease agreements typically include some standard rights and responsibilities of business owners and landlords, also referred to as "terms." For landlords, these generally include (among many others) the right to receive rental payments on time and the responsibility to cover some costs associated with the operation and structural maintenance of the building. For business owners, these generally include (among many others) the right to occupy the premises for a duration of time and the responsibility to pay rent and keep those premises in the condition in which they were leased.

The typical terms a commercial lease covers, however, may vary depending on the location and the type of business or premises concerned. For example, renting space in a prime downtown location will involve different requirements than renting a warehouse in an industrial area, and office, retail, and industrial commercial leases, although all essentially alike, will likely define different terms.

Consequently, because commercial leases place the bulk of responsibility on commercial tenants and strongly favor landlords' interests, it's essential that you understand your rights and responsibilities. Commercial leases for office, industrial, and retail spaces, for example, may specify different types of insurance requirements.

# Understanding Terms

Hiring an attorney to closely examine and explain the terms used in a commercial lease you're considering signing is vital to fully understanding both your own rights and obligations as well as your landlord's.

Commercial leases commonly include terms related to rental rate, rental rate increases, common area maintenance, repairs, alterations to the property and who owns them, options to renew and dates within which to do so, duration of lease, subleases, how the property can be used, nonpayment of rent, options to terminate and dates within which to do so, condition of property upon termination, janitorial services, overtime services (such as utilities rate hikes after hours), and contents and/or repairs insurance.

Before you sign your commercial lease, it is important that you understand its terms and your obligations. If you don't understand the terms, seek legal advice.

# Negotiating Terms

Once you know and understand the terms in the lease, your attorney can help you to negotiate them.

Although all terms in a lease are important and can be negotiated, some of the primary terms to examine and potentially negotiate pertain to rate, repairs, term (duration) of lease, options to renew, options to sublease and assign, and personal guarantee.

Let's look at some of these.

## Base Rent

Base rent is one of the terms small business owners usually look at first because it involves the money that will come out of their pockets on a monthly basis for the duration of the lease. Negotiating rate is therefore an important concern, and the process of doing so is based on many factors, including the demand for the space, location, and what the rate is for similar spaces in locations nearby.

## CAM Charges

Another example is the term "community association maintenance" (CAM) charges. CAM charges are monies that tenants pay to landlords in exchange for the right to share in the use of common spaces. Landlords have expenses related to the maintenance of these shared spaces, so tenants must compensate them for these. CAM expenses vary depending on property type. However, typical CAM charges might include those associated with parking lots, lighting, landscaping, electric, heating and air-conditioning, and property management fees, among many others.

When negotiating rate, therefore, rather than looking solely at base rent costs (as many new small business owners do), you need to also look at these additional costs and ascertain what portion of them you will be responsible for paying.

How do commercial tenants and their landlords do this? Well, each type of lease accounts for CAM charges in its own way. One common lease type (known as the "net lease"), for example, adds the tenant's portion of these charges separately, in addition to base rent. Another common lease type (known as the "gross lease") includes CAM charges in base rent.

Okay, you might be thinking, "Sounds simple enough." Not so fast. There are many more considerations. For one, how do you verify the landlord is actually paying the amounts claimed for these common space expenses? How do you ensure your right to verify claimed expenses is stipulated in the lease? And what else can you negotiate to minimize your contribution toward them?

Although this chapter does not discuss these questions in depth, generally, the most effective way to verify the accuracy of CAM expenses is via an express audit right written into the lease. An express (versus implied) audit right gives the tenant the right to analyze the landlord's books. Determining exactly what this entails, such as who pays for the audit, can get complicated, so having an attorney examine such terms can be of great assistance. Please note, however, that by seeking an audit from the landlord, you may incur additional expenses, and doing so will not foster a good relationship with the landlord. Have a discussion with your attorney prior to exercising this option.

As for negotiating your contribution toward CAM charges, you might, for instance, be able to negotiate a cap on the amount you contribute in your first year in business, negotiate an ongoing cap to ensure that the amount won't increase exorbitantly year over year, and negotiate the exclusion of certain expenses, such as mortgage payments and property management fees.

Other factors upon which rate can be negotiated include (among others) term (duration) of lease, your business record, the type and extent of repairs and/or improvements you commit to making on the property, length of time the property's been empty, local area rental rate, and the property's location and condition. These may all provide opportunity to negotiate a more favorable rate with your landlord. You might, for example, be able to negotiate annual increases in rate, negotiate moving costs into your first year's rate, exclude an increase until after the first year, and/or secure a cap on each subsequent year's increase.

## Option to Renew

The option to renew clause in your commercial lease provides you with the right to extend your lease if you wish to stay on the premises beyond expiration of term. You must, however, abide by the notification deadlines stipulated in the lease. These deadlines, as well as other specific dates in the option to renew clause, can have significant impact on your business and should be carefully considered and negotiated before you sign the lease agreement.

One key to understanding the option to renew clause is to remember that it benefits you, the tenant, more than the landlord. While you might assume that if you're a good tenant, the landlord will be eager to renew your lease and so provide you with good incentive to do so, this is not necessarily the case. Landlords are often eager to bring in new tenants at higher rates, so they may actually be more willing to offer legal or financial benefits to incoming, versus renewing, tenants.

Further, landlords know that it likely will take you a long time and involve considerable expense to find a new location, negotiate a new lease, and possibly add improvements to an alternative space. They are also aware that if you've been in a certain location for a while, you've likely built up a clientele in that area that you're reluctant to risk losing.

It's advisable to forecast your business needs and negotiate your option to renew clause before you sign a commercial lease, rather than to try to renegotiate it once you're already in the space. Tenants who postpone doing so until the expiry of their lease looms on the horizon or who miss the date to give their landlord notice are at a disadvantage, and landlords may try to exact higher rents, add expenses, or renew the lease term for a period that's either too long or short.

One of my clients discovered this the hard way. This client, a consultant, had leased commercial space from his landlord for fifteen years. Over this time, he'd signed three five-year leases. When he attempted to exercise his option to renew clause rights in order to extend the third lease at an annual increase rate of 3 percent, however, even though he'd met the renewal deadline, the landlord responded that he wanted a 25 percent increase, or approximately $1,000 more per month! A closer look on my part at the now fifteen-year-old lease revealed that the percentage increase stipulated was subject to the landlord's "full and absolute discretion," meaning that even though a rate of 3 percent had been agreed to, the landlord could alter it as he chose. Luckily, after reviewing the lease further, I also found a contradictory clause stating that any such discretionary increase must be calculated based on the Consumer Price Index, a calculation that did not accord with an increase of 25 percent. Finding these two contradictory clauses in the lease created an opportunity to either go to court or negotiate an alternative rate. However, had my client and the landlord foreseen the eventuality of needing to exercise his option to renew when they signed the original lease and solicited counsel to help more specifically negotiate it (in other words, to negotiate a rate based on a percentage range rather than "market rate"), this situation could have been avoided.

## Options to Sublease and/or Assign

Options to sublease give tenants the option to transfer portions of the property they themselves have leased from the landlord to a third party. A hairdressing salon might, for example, sublease a portion of the salon to a nail technician to provide a manicure service to clients as the hair salon owner continues to conduct business on the premises. Options to assign give tenants the option to transfer an outstanding balance on a lease term to a third party. A commercial tenant who wants to move before the term of his lease expires, for instance, might wish to do so without being held responsible for continuing to pay rent for that space.

One of the most important things to understand about options to sublease/assign is that both must be accompanied by a landlord's consent clause, or they could be invalid. Most commercial leases stipulate that such consent shall not be unreasonably withheld. However, both tenants and landlords may wish to negotiate the consent's finer points. Tenants, for example, might want to specify what their responsibilities are in the process of subleasing or assigning (such as notifying the landlord and drafting sublease/assignment documents) and to determine what the landlord requires to qualify a third-party tenant (such as financial documentation and/or meeting regulatory requirements for the space).

Failing to ensure landlord's consent prior to either subletting or assigning a third-party tenant can have dire consequences.

Take for example the case of a client of mine, the owner of a retail establishment that sold gifts in a strip mall. This business owner had signed a sublease agreement to rent space from another business owner in the mall who had already signed a commercial lease with a landlord. The sublease stated that my client was responsible for paying rent until the end of a specified term. Before that term expired, though, she decided she wanted to sell the business. When she contacted a business broker to assist her, however, he asked her for a copy of the sublease agreement and found it omitted the landlord's consent.

This was bad news for many reasons. For one, lack of consent made the sublease legally invalid. The gift retailer, now my very distressed client, wasn't entitled to operate on the premises. For another, she couldn't obtain a permit from the municipality to operate. Rather than sell her business, therefore, she had to close it and incur the expense of retaining my counsel to help her sue the business owner who'd created the sublease agreement.

## Personal Guarantee

Another of the most critical terms to examine and negotiate in a commercial lease is the personal guarantee. The term "personal guarantee" means exactly what it sounds like: it's a guarantee that if you don't pay rent when due, the landlord can sue you personally for payment.

Given the high number of small businesses that fail every year, personal guarantees are very common in commercial lease agreements. Landlords want to insulate themselves against the possibility that your business may not succeed. So you will most likely have to agree to one if you sign a commercial lease. However, there are ways to limit your personal responsibility even if you do.

For example, you may negotiate the option to assign (as discussed previously) your lease to a new tenant yourself. This gives you an out should you need to close your business or move to a new location. You may also be able to negotiate sharing the personal guarantee among several people so that if you find yourself unable to pay rent, you will not be solely responsible for continuing to do so.

A limited-time personal guarantee is a possibility. Since the riskiest period of a new business's life is the first two years, a landlord may be open to considering a limited-time personal guarantee, a guarantee that expires after a specified period, as long as all other payments you're responsible for are up to date.

It might also be possible to sign the commercial lease in a corporate capacity, rather than under your personal name. This would mean that should you be unable to pay, only the corporation would be liable for nonpayment.

Finally, you might be able to negotiate a higher security deposit in lieu of signing a personal guarantee.

## Repairs/Improvements

Commercial tenants should understand who is responsible for making repairs to the building itself, the premises the tenant is leasing, and any equipment used on the leased premises and common areas. Generally, landlords are responsible for structural repairs; however, responsibility for making repairs to equipment that serves the leased premises, such as HVAC systems, are usually the tenant's responsibility. As a tenant, for instance, you might be able to negotiate that you are responsible for routine maintenance on such equipment, while the landlord is responsible for replacing it (or any part of it) if necessary. You might also be able to negotiate a rent abatement if the landlord neglects to perform necessary repairs, or if the repairs limit/prevent your use of the premises, as well as to stipulate certain conditions with regard to making repairs, such as that the landlord must do so outside of business hours.

## Additional Charges

Another area in which an attorney is indispensable when you're signing a commercial lease regards charges in addition to the base rent. As noted, business owners often look at the base rent amount stipulated in the lease and assume it comprises their sole—or at least the bulk of—their financial responsibility. Yet, in addition to your base monthly rent (and the aforementioned CAM charges), you may also have to pay some or all of the following: sales tax, insurance, property taxes, percentage of gross sales, and others.

Additional charges, also commonly referred to as "additional rent," in your commercial lease can become nasty surprises, and if there's a contract that has additional rent charges, it's the commercial lease agreement. Keep in mind that commercial properties exist to make money for the landlord, and commercial leases commonly have additional charges, in addition to the base rent. Failure to read the lease thoroughly could create surprises that will likely cost you money. Try to avoid them by doing your due diligence and staying informed.

# Common Oversights

## Oral Agreements

This might sound incredible, but you'd be surprised at the number of business owners who assume an oral agreement will be sufficient to secure their interests in a commercial lease. Even if your landlord *says* she or he agrees to a rate or promises to give you an extra month to pay, to extend the lease by a few months, or to waive penalties for exiting early, *you must put this in writing*. Unfortunately, taking someone's word in matters of business just can't be relied upon. No matter how trustworthy your relationship with your landlord, circumstances change quickly, and when money is involved, people often can't be counted on to honor what they say.

## Compliance

Small business owners considering signing a commercial lease should ensure that the space to be leased complies with federal, state, and local laws, such as the Americans with Disabilities Act. Additionally, tenants should have the landlord confirm the building itself complies with all applicable laws, that the business the tenant plans to operate in the space is not in violation of any laws, and that the condition the landlord leases the space in will not prevent or inhibit any work the tenant needs to do to fit the premises to its business purpose or to obtain any necessary permits to conduct business.

## Duty to Restore

It's important that the lease clearly states tenants' obligations in terms of restoring spaces at the end of lease term or upon early termination. Tenants, for instance, shouldn't be required to remove any improvements they made to the premises under the conditions of the lease or any alterations made during the lease term (as long as the landlord provided consent for such alterations).

Alternatively, if tenants are to be held responsible for restorations, their extent and nature, as well as the dates within which the landlord must provide notice to require, should be specified. Further, any restoration responsibility should exclude reasonable wear and tear on the premises. A tenant, for example, might want to limit restoration responsibility to specific improvements (such as lighting fixtures or specialty features such as water fountains) and to exclude responsibility for reasonable wear and tear on preexisting carpeting, wallpaper, and/or anything the landlord would normally be responsible for repairing.

The terms and negotiation options discussed in this chapter are neither exhaustive nor intended as legal advice that will meet your specific business needs. My point is solely to give you an overview of their variety and to emphasize the necessity of retaining an attorney to help you make sense of and negotiate them.

Signing a commercial lease without benefit of counsel could be one of your costliest mistakes, but if you're still not convinced, consider this: Let's say for example that your monthly lease payment, after all the charges, adds up to $2,500 per month, and the lease has thirty-six months remaining before the next renewal. Upon signing this lease agreement, you just assumed a $90,000 debt with a personal guarantee! Many people come to my office wanting to "get out!!!" of such leases after their businesses go south. Typically, though, there are few, if any, exit clauses on a commercial lease agreement. Keep this in mind as you move forward.

Remember, commercial leases are complex contracts, and there is no one-size-fits-all when it comes to

> EVEN IF YOU DO NOT HIRE A LAWYER FOR ANY OTHER REASON, SIGNING A COMMERCIAL LEASE IS A GOOD REASON TO DO SO.

contracts in general. So *even if you do not hire a lawyer for any other reason, signing a commercial lease is a good reason to do so.* Understanding and negotiating the finer points of your commercial lease agreement before you commit to paying monthly rent for years into the future is as crucial as understanding how you're going to make that money itself—a subject discussed in the next chapter.

## MISTAKE 5

# LACK OF KNOWLEDGE ABOUT HOW THE BUSINESS WILL MAKE MONEY

It's surprising how many prospective business owners do not understand how their business will make money. You can have a great idea, but until you can figure out how it will generate income, it's just that: an idea.

One of my clients discovered this the hard way. This client took out a loan and paid $200,000 to buy an online store. Once he attempted to start making money from the store, however, he learned that the seller had failed to disclose information crucial to his ability to do so: the inventory had expired, some of the store's suppliers no longer provided the products my client had counted on selling, and the financial statements were incomplete. My client, therefore, was out a great deal of money, but he had no knowledge as to how the business he'd just purchased would make any.

A lot of planning needs to be done to understand how your business will make money. You need to know the details of what you're planning to sell, who supplies it, whether those suppliers are still in business or able to supply what your customers want, the expenses you'll incur in bringing product to market, and your break-even points. All my client had done was to base his income projection on a two-year-old gross revenue figure provided by the seller.

Rather than digging deeply into the way a business will make money, many business owners are so eager to get started that, like this client, they put themselves at risk of not being able to do so. This is true whether they're starting or purchasing a business and whether that business involves selling products or services.

Nine times out of ten, clients come to see me at the point at which they're about to sign a commercial lease. They think they're at the beginning stage of starting their business. However, the process of going into business should begin long before that. Therefore, when I meet prospective business owners who want to open a corporation and obtain a trademark to start their new enterprise, I take a step back. My first question to them is, "Tell me about your business."

Most of the time, I receive a long explanation to this question. My clients tell me how the business is going to operate, how it's going to be marketed, and who's going to run it. Not bad, but the first thing I'm hoping to hear is always: How are you going to make money selling this product or service?

This might seem like an unnecessary question with an obvious answer. You have a product or service that there's a demand for, and you intend to sell it. A lot more goes into making money than that, though, and if you do not understand what's involved, you may not be able to pay yourself, the lease, and any obligations, such as payments to vendors, much less make a living.

Further, if you don't make enough money, you may risk legal issues. In fact, I'd go as far as to say that is almost inevitable.

Why? Well, inadequate understanding, based on lack of research and planning, can lead to poor business decisions. If, for example, you have not researched who your customers are or how you are going to market to them, you may make decisions based on false premises. This may lead to insufficient revenue generation, which in turn may lead to legal problems. How? Well, if you don't generate the revenue to pay your expenses, you may not be able to perform the obligations in the contracts you have entered into, which may in turn lead to breach of contract claims.

How thoroughly you understand how your business makes money is, therefore, inextricably intertwined with the potential for legal issues.

## Why People Don't Understand How to Make Money or Its Relationship to Legal Disputes

There are many reasons that would-be small business owners often don't understand how to make money and the relationship of money to the potential for legal disputes.

Many would-be small business owners think passion and having a good product or service is all they need for success. They go into business on an emotional basis because they believe in their product or service and feel it is better than the competition's. Having such passion is fine. Passion provides the motivation to keep going. But it must be coupled with the know-how and solid research to lead to success. So it's important to seek out resources, such as SCORE or a business incubator, that can help you learn more.

Another reason people tend to overlook the importance of understanding how to generate revenues and how not doing so relates to potential legal issues is that rather than their focusing on generating revenue, their motivation for wanting to go into business is being good at something or wanting to escape the need to work for someone else. Neither of these necessarily translates to being proficient at running a business. A mechanic working for a chain of auto repair shops might be very good at fixing transmissions but have little knowledge and experience of incorporating a business and setting up payroll and healthcare for his employees. An artist working for a graphics company might long for the freedom to create her own designs, rather than those her employer needs. Yet even if she's highly talented, and even if she has customers lined up to buy her products, if she's more skilled in her artwork than in balancing her books, she'll likely become one of the 33 percent of small businesses the Small Business Administration reports fail within the first five years. Just because you have an independent streak and/or are technically good at something doesn't mean you'll be good at running a small business.

The good news is that there are many resources available to help you. Attorneys, for example, particularly business attorneys, are well acquainted with the specific areas in which potential business owners need professional guidance. They have the education, experience, and hopefully also the passion to help you plan how you are going to make money and how to protect your business from the types of legal issues that can arise due to lack of funds. Also, it is a good idea to have a capable accountant or CPA on your team right from the start.

Of course, in addition to the services of an attorney, you'll also want to consult other expert resources, such as SCORE, professional trade organizations geared to your industry, your local chamber of commerce, or the Small Business Administration, and/or to take one of the many courses that are becoming available at community colleges that teach you how to access traditional and nontraditional financing options, implement employee-management procedures, and write business policies, among other skills. Attorneys can be very helpful when it comes to setting up both the business and legal infrastructure you need *before* you make your first sale (and certainly before you sign that lease), but that said, the onus is really on business owners to do as much of their own research as possible. Doing so is less costly and provides the basis for a wide range of ongoing decisions. Also, research before start-up is only the first stage of business preparation. Educating oneself is a continual process that should be maintained even while running the business, so as to stay competitive.

# Questions to Consider When Analyzing How Your Business Will Make Money

The question of how to make money in a business involves consideration of many other questions. It's these questions that I usually ask my clients during a consultation. Let's take a look at a few of them.

## Who are your customers?

Even if you have a product or service that's highly necessary and in demand, you can't simply expect that everyone will want to buy your product. You have to define your customer base—not only who your customers are but also their characteristics. Your customer base must be an identifiable group, such as homeowners, students, or people with pets. Further, you must know as many specifics about your identified customer base as possible. You may, for example, want to focus on selling to homeowners with annual household incomes above a certain figure, art students, or exotic pet aficionados. You will need to know these groups' spending habits, where they live, why your product or service suits their particular needs and preferences, and what their education level, age, and occupations are. You might also want to study when they buy. Are they seasonal buyers, on-sale buyers, lunch-break buyers? All of this information will not only help you attract and retain customers, but it will also help you to decide how to market your product in a way that's unique enough to distinguish you from your competitors, where to locate your business, what your operating hours should be, and what types of promotions will be most effective.

## Do you know how to sell?

Selling a product or service isn't as simple as identifying customers and meeting their needs. You also have to know how to build rapport, ask questions, provide answers that are pertinent to the solutions they're looking for, be able to confidently assert your price, and weed out "buyers" who aren't motivated. There is a myriad of resources on selling products and services online that business owners can tap into.

# How much money have you allocated for marketing?

Identifying who your customers are will also help you to decide how much money to allocate to marketing and how to spend your marketing dollar. The US Small Business Administration recommends spending 7 to 8 percent of gross revenues for marketing if you're doing less than $5 million a year in sales and your net profit margin (the money you get to keep after all expenses) is between 10 and 12 percent.[3] While basing your marketing budget on revenues is a neat equation, you also need to consider your specific situation and be flexible. If you've been in business awhile but are launching a new product or service, you may need to spend more than you usually do on marketing to saturate your target market with information about its launch before your competitors catch wind of it. If, however, you're just starting up and don't yet have any revenue on which to base your marketing budget, you might have to spend what you can afford at first, building up your visibility slowly. Many small businesses spend as little as 1 percent on marketing. Indeed, the average across all industries is 1 percent. Retail establishments tend to spend the most, but as the following list shows, research reveals plenty of business types that spend between 1 and 5 percent:

- Furniture stores: 4.44 percent

- Real estate agents: 3.84 percent

- Schools: 2.87 percent

- Home furnishing stores: 2.16 percent

---

3    Will Rico, "How Much Should Small Businesses Spend on Marketing?" *CommonMind*, December 3, 2020, accessed July 23, 2022, https://www.commonmind. com/blog/strategy/small-business-marketing-budget/#:~:text=The%20U.S.%20 Small%20Business%20Administration,percent%20range%20(after%20expenses).

- Personal care services: 1.99 percent

- Restaurants: 1.93 percent

- Specialty food stores: 1.88 percent[4]

There are many factors beyond revenue to consider when you're deciding how much money to allocate to marketing: the stage your business is at—whether you're a start-up or a little more established, your business size and visibility in the market, how many competitors you have and how prominent their marketing is, your marketing plan, and which types of marketing vehicles you need to create maximum sales. An electronic newsletter, for example, may be more cost effective than a billboard; however, if your customers are car owners and your business is a roadside assistance service, your marketing dollar may be best spent on the billboard.

## What is your profit margin?

Generally speaking, the profit margin is the difference between what your product sells for and what it costs you to produce and market it. The profit margin for your small business will depend on how big and what type of business it is. In general, small business owners should aim for a profit margin of between 7 to 10 percent;[5] however, profit margins will fluctuate depending on many of the same factors you consider when deciding how much money to allocate to marketing. There may be seasonal ebbs and flows, for instance. Additionally, as

---

4    George Boykin, "What Percentage of Marketing Revenue Should Be Used for Marketing and Advertising?" *Small Business Chronicle*, March 1, 2019, accessed May 3, 2022, https://smallbusiness.chron.com/percentage-gross-revenue-should-used-marketing-advertising-55928.html.

5    Tim Parker, "What's a Good Profit Margin for a New Business?" *Investopedia*, September 7, 2021, accessed July 7, 2022, https://www.investopedia.com/articles/personal-finance/093015/whats-good-profit-margin-new-business.asp.

your business grows, even though you may be making more sales, your profit margin may decrease to accommodate higher costs for additional staff, warehouse space, and/or whatever other expansion expenses you have.

Understanding your profit margin is important for many reasons, one of them being that it tells you how much money you have to spend somewhere else. So, at the very least, a discussion of how to calculate it, if not a basic course in the subject, is wise.

## Do you have a business plan?

I usually recommend writing a business plan. A business plan is a viable tool to assist you to crystalize your thinking and consider various scenarios before you invest money in a new venture. A business plan is like the foundation of a house. It stabilizes the entire structure of the business, acting as a base upon which to make business decisions that align with it. It also provides a tool with which to leverage funding, showing potential investors how well you've thought through your purpose and goals and how to achieve them. Business plans include a range of detail about your proposed business, including your financials, financial targets, and growth plans; descriptions of the problems your products or services solve; who your customers are; who your competitors are, what they're doing, and why you can do it better; the legal structure of your business; who your partners, suppliers, and subcontractors are; what your marketing plan is; and what revenue streams you have (for example, direct sales, membership fees, or business sidelines). A business plan is always a good idea, because if your business does not work "on paper," it most likely won't work in real life.

# Do you want to incorporate?

The vast majority of small businesses in the United States are sole pro-prietorships.[6] Owned by one person, they have no employees and may not even have a business name. There are, however, many reasons why small business owners may want to incorporate. For sole proprietors, one of the main ones is to separate business assets from personal assets. This is because, as a sole proprietor, should you ever be sued, or should creditors come knocking, you will be personally liable, potentially putting your home, car, and other valuable personal assets at risk.

Starting an LLC is a simple and affordable safeguard against this possibility. It also creates a layer of privacy, as it's the registered agent of the LLC who's on record, not your business or home address. An LLC also provides your business with perceived credibility, as your customers know they're dealing with a corporate entity rather than simply an individual, and it provides potential tax breaks that are unavailable to individuals.

## BENEFITS TO INCORPORATING

Some of the reasons it may be beneficial to form a corporation are as follows:

- Liability—No longer having personal liability for the business. An owner's personal assets cannot be used to pay for corporate debts or liability.

- Privacy—Those who choose to incorporate also benefit from the operation's privacy. In some states, the owners' names are not a matter of public record.

---

6    George Boykin, "What Percentage of Marketing Revenue Should Be Used for Marketing and Advertising?" *Small Business Chronicle*, March 1, 2019, accessed May 3, 2022, https://smallbusiness.chron.com/percentage-gross-revenue-should-used-marketing-advertising-55928.html.

- Capital—Incorporation also may make it easier to raise funds. A corporation can sell interest in the company, unlike a sole proprietorship or partnership.

- Continuity—Corporate entities are also easier to maintain when there is a change in ownership.

- Taxation—Incorporation also brings added tax benefits.

- Equity Splits—Ensure partners understand how equity will be split in the event of dissolution.

- Stock Options—Enable yourself to issue stock options.

- Funding—Enable yourself to acquire funding.

- Business Credit—Enable yourself to acquire business credit.

## Do you need a trademark?

Often, people who come to see me ask me about registering a trademark with the US Trademark Office for a product or business name. A trademark provides legal protection to use the mark as a business name or for specific products, as well as for any logos or symbols that represent them. Think McDonald's Golden Arches or Nike's "Just Do It" slogan. Both are trademarks that instantly bring to mind the businesses and products they symbolize. There are many advantages to acquiring a trademark, including increasing brand recognition, ensuring competitors don't misuse your brand name, and securing exclusive rights to your products and services. Acquiring a trademark requires some research and an application process; however, the process is relatively simple and affordable compared with the expensive process of defending yourself against a trademark litigation lawsuit, should someone decide to copy your idea or infringe your brand's reputation.

Other questions I commonly ask during consultation with clients to help them analyze how their business will make money include the following: Does your business require a license from the state or from a regulatory agency? How are you planning to pay your employees? And how much cash do you have available to support the first three months of business?

For instance, I once met with a husband-and-wife team who were both nurses working for a healthcare staffing agency. Knowing that nursing services were in high demand, especially during COVID, and having experience with staffing agencies themselves, they came to me to discuss opening their own such agency, expecting that were they to do so, they'd immediately be able to start making money. Eager to get started, their initial question for me was thus how to incorporate, but as we began talking (as is so often the case), I realized we needed to take a step back. How were they going to do the recruiting? What would the contracts with the various facilities entail? What insurance requirements, such as workers' compensation and professional liability, had they researched? What regulatory requirements would they have to meet? How would they cover payroll? And did they have a business plan? (As I noted previously, a business plan is key.)

**INSUFFICIENT BUSINESS CAPITAL IS ONE OF THE MOST COMMON REASONS SMALL BUSINESSES FAIL.**

Unfortunately, my clients hadn't yet answered any of these crucial questions, and when they realized that even a small staff of nurses, earning $60-plus an hour, would cost them about $30,000 every two weeks (an amount they did not have in reserve but would have to take out of their 401[k]), their initial enthusiasm for their idea began to wane.

My clients were vulnerable on numerous fronts, most especially perhaps their lack of sufficient business capital. *Insufficient business capital is one of the most common reasons small businesses fail.* While it's true that many new business owners start out on a bootstrap—either because, never having run a business before, they have unrealistic expectations as to sales or don't understand the many costs of starting and continuing to operate their businesses—those who succeed are the exception rather than the rule. In fact, even the most highly successful business owners we frequently hear about in the news have had their share of failures.

Risk is a part of doing business, but it should be calculated risk. In this case, therefore, my advice to these clients was to more thoroughly investigate everything involved in opening the type of business they were envisioning before taking the plunge. For example, I suggested they look at what working capital they would need to run the business effectively in the first year and the expected revenue that they would receive based on the expected payment terms of the facilities that they would be contracting with.

## Do you have a partnership agreement?

Before you enter into a partnership with anyone, I suggest that small business owners enter into a partnership agreement. A partnership agreement is highly recommended even if your partner is a friend or relative, because the potential for disputes between partners is very high.

Take, for instance, the case of another client of mine. A hairdresser for many years, she wanted to buy her partner out and take over the lease. Her plan, however, also involved subleasing part of the space to a barber. She and the barber were going to partner up and share expenses, but he was not going to be on the lease.

This is a typical type of situation small business owners are in when they're considering partnering with others. They enter into a casual arrangement, not realizing the risk that's involved if they don't make the partnership legally binding with a partnership agreement. As a result, they often end up in disputes with each other and anyone else involved.

When I recognized the red flags the hairdresser was presenting, my first task was to begin listing potential issues and prioritizing them. My initial question to her, therefore, was, "Who has the lease?" When I found out it was her ex- (or soon-to-be ex-) partner, my next task was to examine that lease. Then, discovering that the lease had an assignability clause, I asked her whether the barber was going to be on it. When she said no, I had to tell her that her plan wasn't going to work. As discussed in the last chapter, an assignability clause is contingent on the landlord's consent. The barber, therefore, had to be on the lease and could only be added with the landlord's permission.

I then began a deeper analysis of her situation, asking her how much her monthly lease payment would be and how many chairs she had in her salon. She said her lease was $3,000 a month, but the barber would be paying half of that in exchange for using some of her chairs.

At this point, I knew this client was putting herself at high risk of legal issues. For one thing, if she let the barber use her space without being on the lease or receiving the landlord's consent, she risked a dispute with the landlord. For another, even though she thought she stood to save 50 percent of her lease expenses, she had no way to ensure the barber would pay. The barber did not plan on giving up his own shop. He had his own lease payment to make in addition to the $1,500 he'd only verbally agreed to pay the hairdresser. Should he renege on that verbal agreement, she would be responsible for the full $3,000 lease payment, as well as all the insurance. Additionally, she was planning to pay her soon-to-be-ex-partner $40,000 to buy out his share of their business.

To go forward with this plan, the hairdresser needed a partnership agreement, and the barber needed to be added to the lease. Further, had they gone ahead with this plan, both of them would have been breaking the lease.

These are by no means all of the questions I ask in my first client interview with new prospective business owners. Still others include the following:

- How much money are you expecting to make your first year?

- How did you learn this business?

- How are you financing your business?

- Who is going to be responsible for the checking account?

- Who is going to cover the initial expenses, and how do you plan to reimburse these expenses?

- What is the percentage of ownership going to be?

- Who are the vendors who will help you with the business?

- Do you have an accountant?

- Where are you planning to run your business?

- Have you entered into any contracts with anyone as of today related to this business venture?

- How are you planning to sell your product?

- Who else will be helping you with this business?

- Can you handle the technical aspects of your business, or do you need to bring on someone who does?

- Do you know how to collect money once a sale is made?

- Can you keep expenses low enough to make a profit?

- How are you planning to promote your business?

If you are going into business by yourself or with other partners, I encourage you to answer these questions in writing. Don't worry. This is not an aptitude test to tell you if you should go into business. I simply want to challenge you to ask yourself questions that will prompt you to dig deeper and give your business some thought. You won't be able to research and plan for every potential scenario you'll face; planning for a business is not a perfect science, but you'll do so to the best of your ability, which will be some consolation should you encounter a problem.

Again, problems are inevitable. Chances are that even if you have a very successful business, you either will or you've already had a few failures along the way. Or perhaps the business that you're in now is not the one you first envisioned. I personally have had my share of such painful problems (or "learning opportunities," as any small business owner with the resilience to survive must learn to view his or her mistakes).

One of these was in my last business. I believe it provides a useful cautionary tale for many small business owners.

My business was HealthcareRecruitment.com, an online healthcare job board kind of like a Monster.com, but for healthcare. This was back in 1996, when technology wasn't what it is today. Back then, job seekers' access to the jobs database relied on phone lines through dial-up services such as AOL, so using it was a slow process, both for me and for the applicants. In order to make the database more reliable, I signed up with a third-party vendor who promised to provide a more robust platform, which would give my clients and job applicants a better experience.

I therefore signed up (for the low, low price of $5,000 per month) with a company that had the advanced programming expertise to manage the backend operation of my entire business with its own database, which had far more bells and whistles. This completely changed my business model, however, because I no longer owned the technology. So, in 2004, when I decided to sell the company, I found that I didn't own my product in its entirety. I still owned the traffic, the trademarks, and the search engine listings, but the database platform itself was not mine. Consequently, all I could do was to sell the contract versus selling my own technology.

Lesson learned? Whenever you outsource aspects of your business, diversify vendors and have a backup plan. Some businesses use applications that handle every aspect of operations, such as client lists, billing, leads, and email addresses. The demos of such applications look great, and they may be—until the application gets a bug, or that vendor goes out of business, or you want to sell your business, or it's time to upgrade your system and you have to redo everything at once. Today, in my law practice, I have different vendors for marketing, billing, accounting, and data. Everything is separate, and I have redundant systems with seamless integration, so that if one fails, I can easily use a backup.

> **DESPITE ALL THE DIFFICULT TIMES, DISAPPOINTMENTS, WILD RIDES, LONG NIGHTS, UNCERTAINTY, AND TEARS, I WOULDN'T CHANGE THE THRILL OF BUSINESS OWNERSHIP FOR ANYTHING.**

As I said in the introduction to this book, despite all the difficult times, disappointments, wild rides, long nights, uncertainty, and tears, I wouldn't change the thrill of business ownership for anything. I'll say it again because it bears repeating: The sense of freedom and independence that being in business for yourself gives you is truly unmeasurable; the confidence to know that you're able to make a living regardless of how the economy is doing is true freedom. The downside, of course, is that sometimes mistakes are made. Even that, however, can be turned to good purpose: being able to share what I've learned with other people makes my own mistakes feel worthwhile.

That said, it is easier (and less expensive) to learn from others' mistakes rather than your own! You don't want to start with a handicap because you didn't consult a professional to help you. Had I myself done so before I started my healthcare recruiting business, I might not be telling you this story today.

# Why Businesses Fail

As mentioned earlier in this chapter, according to the SBA, "33 percent of small businesses fail within the first five years." The reality is the failure rate is much worse. The SBA also finds that only "about half of all establishments survive five years or longer," and only "about one-third survive 10 years or longer."[7]

Why do so many small businesses fail? In my opinion, it's not only lack of planning and lack of understanding as to how to make money but also lack of understanding about how to turn an idea into a system to generate income. Running a business is less about what product or service you're selling and more about building systems, teams, strategies, plans, processes, and forecasts.

*At the end of the day, you are in business to make money. Everything else is secondary.* As a business owner, you have to know how your business will make money. Not doing so will likely lead to legal issues. So, before you go into a business venture, be able to articulate how you will be able to achieve that first sale and get that first check, not

---

7    "Frequently Asked Questions about How Small Business Makes Money," US Small Business Administration Office of Advocacy, August 2018, accessed May 3, 2022, https://www.sba.gov/sites/default/files/advocacy/Frequently-Asked-Questions-Small-Business-2018.pdf.

only so that you'll survive financially but also so that you'll minimize the potential for legal issues.

The questions you need to ask yourself prior to starting a business are so simple, yet so often overlooked—as, unfortunately, are the questions in our next chapter, entering into partnerships without a partnership agreement.

## MISTAKE 6

# ENTERING INTO PARTNERSHIPS WITH FRIENDS AND RELATIVES WITHOUT A PARTNERSHIP AGREEMENT

Partnerships are businesses formed by two or more people who share all profits, debts, losses, and liability.

There are many advantages to business partnerships, a primary one being that you may be able to accomplish more in a shorter period of time with a partner than going it alone. Partnerships, however, also involve some risks. One of them is that should you and your partner disagree about something (and all relationships entail disagreements), the partnership can quickly go south. When this happens, if you don't have a written partnership agreement, it can lead to complicated, distressing, and costly legal issues.

**IF YOU DON'T HAVE A WRITTEN PARTNERSHIP AGREEMENT, IT CAN LEAD TO COMPLICATED, DISTRESSING, AND COSTLY LEGAL ISSUES.**

Take, for example, the case of two friends who started a travel agency. Because they'd known each other for so long, they trusted each other. So they didn't feel they needed a partnership agreement, and indeed, their business operated successfully for twenty years before a conflict arose between them to make them regret this.

The dispute concerned one partner's contention that the other was stealing money from the company. The accusing partner then proceeded to take clients away from the company and shut the other partner out of the computer system, so by the time this client consulted me for help, these two former friends were no longer speaking to each other. What ensued was a lengthy and costly litigation process, which, although we were eventually able to resolve it, could have been avoided had they simply had a partnership agreement with a dispute-resolution clause (I'll talk more about dispute-resolution clauses a little later in the chapter).

During the course of my practice, I have represented many such clients, clients who entered into partnerships without a partnership agreement and lived to regret it.

# Common Types of Partnership Disputes

Some of the most common claims I see with business partnerships involve partners embezzling money from the company, partners changing the locks to the business so other partners cannot enter, and partners using corporate funds for personal use. Partnership disputes between friends and relatives are also frequent, and therefore going into business with people you're close to in your personal life is a high-risk proposition unless a partnership agreement is in place. I have seen lifelong friendships destroyed over business partnerships gone wrong and family relationships strained or severed when a business fails, or when one partner believes trust was violated by the other.

Along with embezzlement, lockouts, and using corporate funds for personal use, there are many other types of common partnership disputes, including the following:

- Breach of contract

- Fraud

- Violation of confidentiality regarding business information

- Disputes about financial management

- Shareholder disputes

- Misappropriation of funds

- Conflicts about workload

- Disagreements about how to use resources

- Misunderstandings regarding roles and authority

This list is by no means comprehensive, as the variety of types of partnership disputes covers the range of issues that characterize relationships in general. In my experience, disputes arise between partners when they feel ignored, angry, or betrayed. However, the types of issues that can arise in business partnerships are as varied and complex as the people involved, and if personal relationships are also at stake, they can become extremely difficult to resolve.

# Types of Partnership Agreements

There are three types of partnerships: general, limited, and partnerships within limited liability corporations.

A general partnership gives all partners equal control over the company and its debts. Additionally, while it enables each partner to act individually on behalf of the business, all partners are responsible for the decisions individual partners make. If, for example, one partner decides to take out a business loan, all other partners will be held responsible for paying back that loan.

Limited partnerships work differently. A limited partnership includes some general partners and some limited partners. A general partner runs the company and is liable for the partnership, while limited partners act as investors, do not run the company, and are not liable for any debts the company incurs.

A limited liability company (LLC) is a company that protects its owners, who can be partners in a business, from personal responsibility for debts and liabilities. LLCs combine the characteristics of a partnership with a corporation. You can be partners within an LLC, but the LLC shields you from personal liability for corporate acts.

It's always advisable to consult an attorney to help you make the decision as to which type of partnership best suits you and your business. And (you guessed it), no matter which type you enter, entering into a partnership agreement is a good idea.

# Steps to Prepare for Partnership

If you are contemplating entering into a partnership, you'll want to keep the following suggestions in mind:

- Have an attorney draft a partnership agreement

- Decide how to fund the business

- Define areas of responsibility

- Ensure all partners have equal access to the company's bank records

- Have a clear procedure regarding authorization of payments from the checking account and use of corporate credit cards

- Use a third-party accounting firm to keep the books

- Use a third-party payroll firm to do payroll

- Keep minutes of meetings and adhere to corporate formalities (i.e., annual meetings of directors and shareholders)

- Have a written agreement on how each of the partners will be compensated

- Outline a clear method for resolving disputes

- Have an exit plan if one of the members wants to leave the partnership

Let's discuss some of these in more detail.

## Have a partnership agreement

Many of the legal disputes I see involve partners with personal relationships who do not have a partnership agreement. Business owners dealing with friends and relatives tend to be more relaxed with formalities such as contracts than when dealing with business associates. While you might feel a partnership agreement is unnecessary given the close relationship, the reality is that a partnership agreement is more likely to keep the peace and maintain the friendship. Whether your relationship with your partner(s) is personal or not, however, having a partnership agreement protects everyone involved from misunderstandings.

## Drafting the partnership agreement

The process of drafting an agreement should not be intimidating. When I receive a request to draft an agreement, I first recommend my clients prepare a list of the items they've already agreed upon and would like to see in the agreement. Next, I send a series of questions that will help me complete the first draft of the agreement. Once drafted, the agreement goes through various revisions, during which, if possible, each partner should have separate counsel to ensure everyone's interests are objectively accounted for.

In addition to the items listed previously, a key item that must be included in the agreement is who has the authority to make independent decisions regarding the operation of the business and when those decisions are to be made. Depending on what type of business you are in, each partner should have some authority to make independent decisions regarding day-to-day operations within his or her area of expertise and responsibility. Major decisions that could have long-term impact on the business, however, should be joint decisions. Remember, you want to go into a partnership because together you can achieve more than if you were running the business alone. Therefore, some flexibility, common sense, and trust should apply when deciding who can do what and when.

## Decide how and when the business will be funded

If there is a potential land mine for litigation between business partners, it is how and when the business will be funded. Usually, one partner has the funds and the other the business know-how.

To avoid funding issues, you need to address at least three crucial points:

- Decide early on if the funds contributed to the business will be considered a capital contribution (or initial investment) toward the business or if they will be considered a loan that has to later be repaid by the company. It's extremely important to clarify this upfront in writing, and it should be included in the partnership agreement.

- Determine each partners' percentage of ownership. Is it going to be fifty-fifty or a different formula?

- Finally, decide how and when distributions will be paid.

## Clearly define areas of responsibility

Defining areas of responsibility is not usually an area of contention for business partners. It's wise, however, to clarify what each of you expects from the other in terms of time and effort devoted to the business. Work hours, time off, areas of independent decision-making authority, when partners can enter into contracts with third parties on behalf of the business, whether hiring and/or other decisions will be made jointly or by one partner, which partner will make such decisions, and what the chain of command will be as new employees are hired are all areas of responsibility that, if not addressed upfront, could create conflicts that may lead to legal issues down the line.

## Have equal access to the bank and financial records of the company

It's heartbreaking when clients come into my office claiming a partner has removed them from the checking account, eliminating their access to the business. If this happens to you, please contact an attorney in your area immediately who can advise you as to how to proceed.

Whenever you open a checking account with a business partner, your first step should be to go to the bank and open it *together*, making sure you're both included as signatories to the account. Further, all partners should receive duplicates of every bank statement and conduct a monthly accounting of how the money was spent.

## Have a clear procedure on authorization of payments from the checking account and use of corporate credit cards

The opportunity to abuse a corporate debit or credit card is very high in small businesses. A very common claim I see in partnership disputes is that one partner used the corporate credit card for personal use. This usually becomes an issue when the relationship goes sour, and one partner is looking for reasons to sue the other. Corporate and personal credit cards should be kept separate, and corporate cards should be used only for items related to the business. You and your partner can agree to a corporate budget and (after speaking with a tax advisor who can inform you as to their tax treatment) allocate certain items used in the business that it will cover. The budget might, for example, cover gas, mobile phone, some travel expenses, and lunch meetings with clients. This will ensure you don't face any surprise charges on your corporate credit card statement (or at least that, if you do, you can seek compensation).

In short, when it comes to use of the corporate credit card, the bottom line is this: make sure before anyone uses it that the items it's to be used for are stipulated in writing. Further, if at some future date you need to modify those items, make sure that's in writing too.

## Hire an accounting firm

Hiring an accounting firm is a good idea because doing so provides a neutral, third-party service that's independent from the daily operations of your business and partners' personalities. An accounting firm can help you with all financial details, such as payroll, bookkeeping, monthly profit-and-loss statements, and cash-flow reports.

Your contract with the accounting firm should include a provision that all partners have equal access to these reports.

## Hire a third-party payroll company

If you don't hire an accounting firm, at least hire a third-party payroll company to run your payroll. The cost to use these companies is negligible compared to the potential fines by the IRS or a state taxing authority for failure to pay the correct amount of payroll taxes and submit the required reports.

## Keep minutes of meetings and adhere to corporate formalities (i.e., annual meetings of directors and shareholders)

Small businesses commonly overlook adherence to corporate formalities, such as holding annual meetings of shareholders and directors. If the business is owned by a husband and wife or by just a few owners, it's easy to postpone or neglect holding such meetings so you can deal with the more immediate matters that arise during daily operations. Running a small business, however, is sort of like keeping a train from going off the tracks. If you don't examine those tracks and make necessary adjustments now and then, the train may derail. It's therefore generally a good idea to schedule meetings with your partner(s), director(s), and/or shareholder(s), either periodically or at least once a year. Doing so will provide opportunity to discuss how the business is doing and make sure you're progressing toward your goals. A memorandum of each meeting should also be drafted so it can be referred to later. Such memorandums (even if merely in the form of an email summarizing the meeting's key points) can be extremely beneficial, helping you align your business with financial and other goals and providing evidence in the event that a dispute arises over who said what and/or whose responsibility it is to perform tasks discussed therein.

## Have a written agreement as to how each of the partners will be compensated

Compensation is usually a sensitive subject between partners and a ripe area for potential lawsuits. The conflict usually arises when one partner believes he or she deserves to be compensated more than the other. Perhaps the partner believes she devotes more hours to the business, brings in more clients, and/or possesses specialized skills to produce goods or deliver services. These are all good reasons to want to be compensated fairly. However, there's no rule that states how much each partner should be paid; that's up to you and your partner(s).

When compensation is unclear and one partner begins to pay him- or herself out of the corporate checking account, it adds fuel to the fire, likely leading to an implosion in the form of a lawsuit. Whatever arrangement you make regarding compensation, as well as when and how it will be paid and any benefits it includes, should therefore be specified in writing and signed by both parties. As with all written documentation, such agreements aren't written in stone. They can be amended over time and as business conditions change. They are, though, essential safeguards to put in place before you enter the partnership.

**IT'S IMPORTANT TO BE PREPARED FOR THE POSSIBILITY OF A DISPUTE.**

## Have a method for resolving disputes

As in most personal relationships, it's not uncommon to have disagreements from time to time. In a business partnership, you can expect to have these disagreements, too, and sometimes they're as fraught with conflict as they often are in divorce proceedings. Don't get caught up in a War of the Roses situation. It's important to be prepared for the possibility of a dispute, so I recommend including a method for resolving them in your partnership agreement to make their resolution as stress-free and inexpensive as possible.

Your approach to resolving disputes is key. Disputes don't necessarily have to turn into lawsuits. They can, instead, be used to find solutions to problems, identify necessary changes, and boost trust between parties by showing them they can collaboratively and successfully resolve challenges.

Taking this attitude sets a cooperative tone for your partnership and, if written into the partnership agreement, may ultimately provide a faster, less costly, and less stressful way of dealing with a dispute should one arise. Rather than assuming, for example, that resolving conflict will involve filing a lawsuit, you might stipulate that negotiation, mediation, arbitration, or even just a cooling-off period be tried before you address the issue in court.

Your local counsel will be able to advise you on which alternative dispute-resolution option is most suitable for you.

## Have an exit plan in case one of the partners wants to leave the partnership

Business partnerships don't last forever, and for a variety of reasons, one or more of the partners may want to leave the business and "cash out."

Business partnerships end for many reasons. In some instances, a partner may wish to retire or pursue new options. In others, partners may feel their ideas for the business are going in different directions, or one partner might believe the other is not meaningfully contributing to the enterprise. Circumstances can also arise in which partners cannot agree on issues that are essential to running the business. Two friends, for example, may go into business together only to find they have different work ethics or are otherwise incompatible in a business relationship. Not every business venture is meant to last, and it's important to recognize when a partnership is in decline.

I frequently counsel clients who own shares in a business and want out, and my first question in such situations is whether they have a partnership or shareholder's buy-sell agreement. Most of the time, the answer is no. Further, when I ask how much their shares are worth, the answer I most frequently receive is "I don't know."

You and your partner may have spent years building your business, but when it's time to cash out, unless you know its value, you'll likely fail to reap the full financial benefits. If you are interested in leaving the partnership or would like to buy out your partner, I recommend having an idea of what the business is worth.

This situation can be avoided by planning for exit. Your partnership agreement should include a provision stipulating how your percentage of ownership will be valued, as well as how, when, and to whom you can sell your shares. Again, this is very important, yet it is often unaddressed.

Remember, this provision is only a fallback plan to ensure at least the specified amount in the event that you and your partner(s) do not agree on the purchase price. You can always agree to sell your shares for a different amount than the formula on the agreement. Having the formula worked out in advance can save you time and money in the future—and it can avoid a potential legal dispute.

## Have a plan in the event that a partner dies

The death of a partner can be a distressing and unexpected disruption to your partnership. A partnership agreement can, however, prepare you for such a situation by stipulating what happens to your deceased partner's share in the business. Usually, it transfers to a surviving spouse or other family member by way of that partner's will. This means you may be in a position of either taking that person on as a partner or attempting to buy them out, transitions that can create serious issues for you if you don't prepare for them in a partnership agreement.

## Other types of partnership mistakes

Beyond those partnership mistakes listed previously, there are many other types of mistakes that partners in a business should try to avoid.

### FAILING TO ASSESS PARTNERS' STRENGTHS AND WEAKNESSES

The first of these is failing to assess the individual strengths and weaknesses of each partner. One of the advantages of partnership is that it offers a wider talent pool. However, partners should assess their respective talents before going into business together. The assessment should ensure they have the skills and credentials the business needs, as well as confirm their skills and approaches to doing business are complementary. One partner, for example, might be good at sales, while another partner is good at operations. One partner might be an idea person, while the other is more hands-on.

Identifying what each partner does and does not bring to the table before forming the partnership helps to assess the long-term sustainability of the partnership, increases the likelihood that partners will be able to successfully collaborate toward shared goals, and decreases the potential for one partner to take more credit than is warranted for his or her own contribution. A partner who's good with people, loves sales, and brings in most of the business, for instance, is less likely to feel she's carrying the bulk of the business if she recognizes the other partner is great with managing supply chains, handling advertising, and dealing with technology.

## INADEQUATELY CAPITALIZING YOUR BUSINESS

Inadequately capitalizing your business is a likely route to issues. It's important to project cash flow, revenue, and expenses to ensure you'll have sufficient funds. One of the common problems that arises when businesses are not adequately capitalized, for example, is the necessity to pay a partner or employee before a sale is finalized. If you don't have adequate capital to cover payroll, you may have to resort to using other financing sources, such as business loans, which could be very costly.

## NEGLECTING TO KEEP ADEQUATE PAYROLL RECORDS

Neglecting to keep payroll records is a mistake no business owner wants to make. I recently had a case in which my client was sued for overtime pay. Unfortunately, because he had not kept adequate payroll records, he had to pay unpaid wages and penalties. As a business owner, it is your responsibility to keep adequate records, and if you do not have them, it will be presumed that the employee is right. With today's electronic record-keeping software, it's relatively straightforward to keep payroll records up to date.

## FAILING TO CONSIDER POTENTIAL LIABILITY ISSUES

Additionally, consider potential liability issues. As previously noted, if you form a general partnership, all partners may be liable for business debts and obligations, and each partner may be liable for the actions of the other. If you are considering entering into a partnership, it is important to consider all the pros and cons with your legal counsel prior to signing the partnership agreement.

# Final Thoughts Regarding Partnerships

It's not my intention to discourage you from entering a partnership. The reality is that to be successful in business, you have to collaborate with others, and again, you may find that partnerships and joint ventures can help you achieve your goals faster than going solo.

Some of the many advantages of partnerships include access to more capital and human resources, greater borrowing capacity, potential tax savings, moral support, and having a partner to pick up the slack should you be ill for a time or wish to go on vacation. It's also relatively easy to set up a partnership and to change the business structure should you wish to at some future date.

Further, not all partnership conflict is so major that it results in lengthy legal battles or even the dissolution of your business. Some disputes are relatively minor. While even minor conflicts may slow down revenue generation by interrupting business flow (the daily process you've created to acquire customers, provide service, and collect revenue), my message here isn't to avoid partnership so much as to prepare for it by protecting yourself.

Don't be afraid of partnering with others. Just be clear about your objectives and assertive when you perceive problems, and before you form any partnership, have an attorney draft a partnership agreement. Many of the legal problems that arise from partnerships are preventable if you take this necessary precaution, because partnership agreements go a long way to avoiding misunderstandings.

Misunderstandings (or lack of understanding in general), of course, are not only the source of many partnership disputes; they're also the source of many business mistakes in general. We'll see this in the next chapter, in which we discuss lack of understanding of basic contract law.

## MISTAKE 7

# LACK OF UNDERSTANDING OF BASIC CONTRACT LAW

Some time ago, a client of mine asked me to review a contract, a commercial lease agreement, that she was considering signing. This lease agreement contained terms (as all contracts do) that my client didn't understand. Consequently, she didn't clearly know what her rights and obligations would be should she sign it. It wasn't until I clarified its terms for her that she was able to determine whether the contract reflected her needs and goals in opening a business. Had she not consulted with me and instead signed the lease without adequately understanding it, she might have faced some unpleasant and costly issues later on.

As a business owner, you don't need to know the complexities of contract law. You do, however, need to know a few basics. This chapter outlines some of them. As with all other chapters in this book, it doesn't constitute legal advice about your particular situation, but it generally covers what is, in my opinion, the most essential information you need to know before entering into a contract.

# What Is a Contract?

In layman's terms, a contract is simply an agreement between two or more parties that imposes obligations on the parties in the contract.

The following formula can be used to define the term "contract":

**Offer + Acceptance + Consideration = Contract**

As a business owner, you should understand that an offer means an invitation to do something, based on certain terms and conditions, in exchange for something of value. The acceptance is the agreement to that invitation, and the consideration is the "something of value," such as money, property, a service, or a stipulation that you give up a right that you otherwise had. All three are essential for the formation of a binding contract.

For example, once you have selected a location for your business, the landlord or property manager gives you a lease agreement with the terms of the lease for your review. That is the offer. If you agree with its terms (such as the monthly rent, length of the lease, and the other provisions), you go ahead and sign the lease (the acceptance) and pay the first month and security deposit (the consideration). By fulfilling these three elements, you have entered into a binding contract.

# Meeting of the Minds

It is important to remember that before signing any binding contract, all parties should reach a "meeting of the minds" with regard to its terms. This means that all parties, after discussing those terms, should agree both about what they mean and that the language used in the contract reflects their shared interpretation.

Unfortunately, people often think they have a meeting of the minds, but they don't. Very commonly, this happens when they're buying and/or selling a business. They verbally "agree" on the terms, then consult with me or another attorney to review them. More often than not, there is a discrepancy regarding what they believe the deal should be and what the documents state. I then have to go through the interview process with the client.

Remember this: Whenever you have an undefined term in a contract, or anything else that's not finalized, you don't have a meeting of the minds. Therefore, you don't have a contract.

# Importance of Having an Attorney Help You Draft and/or Revise a Contract

If you're drafting a new contract, reevaluating an old one, or reviewing one (especially one prepared by someone else's attorney), it's very important to have an attorney's help.

When you work with an attorney experienced in contract law, it will help you to understand the contract's essential terms—those key words and phrases that define the subject matter of the contract, the parties' intent, the duration of contract, and many other specifics of the agreement, such as the obligations of each party.

The attorney will also examine the contract's provisions regarding how the parties are to handle certain situations, should they arise. For example, a provision as to dispute resolution might specify whether conflicts are to be addressed in court or through mediation, as well as who will pay for legal expenses.

Additionally, an attorney should ensure that the contract abides by applicable state or federal laws. If, for example, you've downloaded a standard online contract, an attorney can customize it as required by such local laws and as necessary to the unique needs of your business.

# Importance of Having an Attorney Help You Interpret a Contract before You Sign

Once all parties involved have come to a meeting of the minds, you'll need an attorney to interpret the contract before you sign it.

Many of the reasons this is a good idea are the same as those discussed previously with regard to drafting and/or revising the contract. However, there are some additional reasons to consult with an attorney at this stage:

- If you're considering entering a contract prepared by another party's counsel, you are already at a disadvantage, and you'll benefit by having your own attorney look it over with solely your own interests in mind.

- By the time the contract is ready to be signed, there may be changes to state and local laws and/or to industry regulations that need to be incorporated. Laws and regulations change frequently, and an attorney who keeps abreast of them can make sure your contract complies with them.

- Legal jargon used in contracts can be confusing. An attorney can ensure you understand it before you sign anything you are not clear about, ensure no critical terms are omitted, and check the accuracy of any industry terms.

- An attorney can review the contract with an eye to closing any legal loopholes that might leave you open to liability.

- An attorney can advise you of any additional contracts you may need to draft and sign. As we will soon discuss, business owners deal with many types of contracts, and you need an attorney with the experience to understand what these are and how they work together.

- Finally, an attorney can make sure the contract protects you against a potential breach, as best as possible.

# Types of Questions Your Attorney May Ask before Drafting and during Contract Review

Many questions need to be addressed before you enter into a contract, as it's very important that you understand what the contract requires you to do and whether it matches what you are trying to accomplish.

Some of the questions I ask clients before drafting a contract and/ or while reviewing it include the following:

- Who are the parties?

- How do you know the parties?

- Do the parties exist (corporation, LLC)?

- Are the parties legal entities?

- What are the contract's terms?

- Can you tell me about the deal or business arrangement?

- Who extended the offer?

- Who accepted the offer?

- How was the offer accepted?

- Who has the legal authority to sign the contract?

Let's look at some of these questions:

## Who are the parties? How do you know them? Do they exist? Are they legal entities?

For instance, one of my clients approached me regarding reviewing a joint venture agreement. When I looked up the entity she was considering entering into contract with, however, it did not exist. In other words, it had no legal entity! Now, maybe this "company" was about to be formed, or maybe it was in the process of being created, but that was no comfort to my client, who, quite understandably, decided not to proceed with the agreement.

As a savvy business owner, you should know who you are doing business with. In this era of transparency, there are very few secrets, and it's not difficult to find a great deal of information about anyone. If you're going to enter into a contract with a company you have not heard of before, you should at least do a Google search, check their corporate status in their state of incorporation, run a quick search on their officers and directors, and have some familiarity with the people you are doing business with.

**AS A SAVVY BUSINESS OWNER, YOU SHOULD KNOW WHO YOU ARE DOING BUSINESS WITH.**

The extent of research and due diligence you will need to do to find out who exactly you're dealing with is directly proportional to how involved they will be in your business. If you're considering entering a one-time or routine transaction, then a limited amount of due diligence may be necessary. However, if the transaction involves a substantial exchange of funds and/or a long-term commitment, do your homework. My advice is to follow your instincts. If a contemplated business transaction keeps you up at night because something "seems wrong," your instincts are probably right, and you should stay away from it.

## What are the contract's terms?

While part of an attorney's role is to ensure the parties involved can be identified and are legal entities, another part is to examine and clarify the contract's terms. I therefore also ask questions such as what my clients expect to receive as a result of entering into contract and what they expect to have to give. Only once terms relating to this exchange are understood can the contract be drafted or revised to meet all parties' needs.

In the opening anecdote to this chapter, for instance, I related the story of the client who asked me to review a commercial lease. One of the terms she didn't understand was "net lease." As discussed in chapter 4, a net lease is a lease that adds the tenant's proportional share of operating expenses (such as community association management fees), as well as real estate taxes and insurance, separately, instead of rolling them into the base rent. Had I not explained that her financial obligation therefore included not only the base rent amount stipulated in the contract but also several other charges, she would not have been aware of her responsibility to pay them. Imagine signing a years'-long contract expecting to receive a space for a specified amount, then discovering that you owe extra money every month!

## Can you tell me about the deal or business arrangement?

Another reason you'll want to have a clear understanding of the terms of the contract is to be able to evaluate whether the contract mirrors your understanding of the business arrangement. Consequently, I also ask my clients to share details of why they are considering entering into this contract and how they anticipate the business arrangement will work.

Most of my clients enter into agreements to either make or save money. Asking the client to articulate the contemplated business proposal, therefore, helps me understand if she or he has a true understanding of how *specifically* that will happen. I consequently spend a good amount of time asking questions about the business deal and the people involved—so much so that, I confess, my clients sometimes grow frustrated.

Why do I risk frustrating my clients with such questions? The answer is this: because I've seen too many good and honest businesspeople being taken advantage of by dishonest operators or making big financial mistakes. My goal is to protect my clients and raise the necessary red flags to keep them from losing a great deal of money. Neglecting to perform due diligence and asking the right questions will likely lead to doing just that. So, when you're considering entering into a contract, curb your enthusiasm! If the deal you're contemplating contains any of the following characteristics, take a step back and reconsider:

- Deals you need to sign right away or by a certain date

- Deals that require you to deposit money into someone's "escrow" account immediately

- Deals with other parties or companies about which there is limited information

- Deals in which the other party threatens to "walk out"

- Deals that require cash payments

- Deals in which one of the parties refuses to provide due diligence information

- Deals in which the terms change frequently as new information becomes available

## Who extended the offer? Who accepted the offer? How was the offer accepted?

As I ask my clients for their version of the events that led to the formation of the deal, one of the things I'm looking for is if there's both an offer and acceptance and if there was a meeting of the minds. If you remember the formula:

**Offer + Acceptance + Consideration = Contract**

Let's discuss this in more detail. Say, for example, you would like to purchase online advertising for your business in a local directory. You speak with the representative and say you'd like to purchase a series of ads to advertise your business over the next ten weeks. The representative sends you a contract with the rate of $300 per week for the next ten weeks, for a total of $3,000. You then read the contract, cross out $300, write in $250 for the next eight weeks, and sign the contract. Do you have a contract? No. Why? You rejected the offer of $300 per week and changed the terms of the original offer.

Rather than a contract, what you have instead is a "counteroffer." A counteroffer acts as both a rejection of the original offer and a new offer that materially alters its terms. The sales rep would have to accept your changes to have a contract.

Every time you issue a counteroffer, rejecting the original offer, that original offer is off the table. You cannot return to it if your counteroffer is rejected. Keep this in mind when you are negotiating, because, again, to form a contract, you must have a valid offer, an acceptance, and a consideration.

## Who has the legal authority to sign the contract?

You also need to make sure the person you're dealing with has the authority to enter into the business transaction you're contemplating. Corporations work through agents. There may, for example, be a salesperson involved in the signing of the sales order; however, a salesperson won't necessarily have the authority to sell the company or make any purchases on its behalf. If a vendor drops by a restaurant to deliver supplies, for instance, and a cashier or other staff member without the legal authority to sign for them does so, that cashier's "apparent" authority (in other words, the vendor reasonably inferred the cashier is acting on behalf of the business owner) means that the contract could be binding on the business owner.

# Breach of Contract

An adequate understanding of basic contract law should also include an understanding of what constitutes breach of contract.

Essentially, a breach of contract is a failure to perform the material obligations outlined in the contract. A breach of contract can occur when one party in a contract unjustifiably fails to meet his or her obligations as specified by the contract. Breach can also occur when a party violates the contract by preventing another party from fulfilling their obligations.

Breach of contract is one of the most common types of disputes between business owners, and some of its most frequent forms include failing to pay or to pay on time, delivering poor quality goods or services, failing to finish a job, or failing to deliver goods or services.

One of my clients, for example, purchased $30,000 of office supplies from a vendor who, after accepting my client's payment, never delivered them. Another of my clients paid a contractor a deposit to remodel her home. The contractor took the funds but never did the work.

When a breach of contract occurs, the person who suffered the breach is entitled to sue the party who caused it for a remedy. This remedy might take the form of monetary compensation (termed "damages"), or it might be a cancellation of the contract (also known as "rescission"), and it places the party in the original position, as if the contract was never entered into in the first place.

I frequently counsel potential clients who would like to file suit for breach of contract, asking some of the questions discussed previously, as well as some of those that follow:

- What were your obligations under this agreement?

- What were the other party's obligations?

- How did the other party breach the contract?

- Where is the other party located (city, state, country)?

- If the contract is written, does it have provisions for attorney fees?

- What were your losses as a result of this alleged breach? How did you arrive at that number?

- How much money do you want to recover?

- How much would you settle for right now?

- How much are you prepared to spend in legal fees to enforce this contract?

- Who extended the offer?

- Who accepted the offer?

- Does the person who accepted the offer have the authority to accept on behalf of the corporation or entity?

- How was the offer accepted?

- Was any money exchanged as a result of this agreement?

- Were any services performed as a result of this agreement?

- Did anyone change their position as a result of this agreement (i.e., disclose confidential information or trade secrets)?

- Did anyone refrain from doing something they otherwise could have done?

- Was the agreement in writing or oral?

- Why do you think you had a contract?

- Was the agreement developed through a series of email discussions?

Let's look at some of these questions:

## DID ANYONE CHANGE THEIR POSITION AS A RESULT OF THIS AGREEMENT?

A change of position occurs when the parties sign a contract agreeing to certain terms and obligations, and then one of the parties acts in reliance on the contract. For instance, Mary signs an employment agreement with ABC company, and as part of the contract, she is to be paid her relocation expenses across the country. She quits her existing job, packs up her belongings, moves with her family to a new state, and incurs more than $10,000 in moving expenses. On her first day of work, however, her boss tells her that the company will not be paying her relocation expenses. Consequently, Mary should be able to recover them, since she "changed her position" by relying on the contract, which promised that they would be paid. Another example of a change of position might involve, say, the owner of a wedding-planning business who contracted with a couple to organize their wedding party, renting a hall, hiring caterers, and purchasing floral arrangements, only to find, at the last minute, that the couple has decided not to get married and does not want to pay for the wedding planner's services. In such cases, the change in position will likely constitute a breach of contract.

### DID ANYONE REFRAIN FROM DOING SOMETHING THEY COULD HAVE DONE?

Say you're going to sell your business. You sign a contract that obligates the buyer to pay a deposit, so during the time that you're under contract, you can't accept any other offers. You're therefore refraining from doing something that you otherwise could be doing, because if it weren't for that contract, you potentially could sell your business to another buyer. If the buyer then decides against buying the property, he or she has cost you that opportunity.

# The Importance of Timing in Signing Contracts

Business deals are organic, and timing is a factor in their success. If you wait too long for everything to be worked out to the last detail, the deal may not happen; if you move too quickly, you can lose your shirt.

A good business attorney should recognize this and draft a contract to help you achieve your goals within an appropriate time frame. At the very minimum, an attorney can draft a preliminary agreement on what has been agreed upon to date, thereby safeguarding your interest while the rest of the details are worked out. Additionally, when entering into a contract, you would be in better shape if you make sure there's a deposit, a service, or a change in position in order to make the agreement binding.

## Obligations under the Agreement

It's very important that you understand what your own and the other party's obligations are under the agreement. This might appear to be common sense; however, I am frequently asked to review drafts of contracts that do not include specifics regarding the who, what, when, where, and how of the obligations they entail. It is therefore crucial to be able to comprehend and articulate what you're supposed to do when the contract is signed and what you will receive in return.

To ensure this, I often recommend that clients write the terms of the contract in point form. Notating each obligation as a bullet point helps both parties identify them more easily than when they're written in "legalese." The rule of thumb with contracts is to "keep it simple," and a list with bullet points achieves this.

## Types of Contracts

There are many different types of contracts small business owners encounter. Some of these may include the following:

- Licensing agreements

- Promissory notes

- Employee contracts

- Noncompete agreements

- Bill of sale contract

- Partnership agreements

- Indemnity agreement

- Property equipment and lease agreement

- Insurance policies

- Nondisclosure agreement

- Intellectual property contracts

# Common Contract Mistakes

Along with lack of understanding of basic contract law, there are several other mistakes that small business owners commonly make when dealing with contracts. Hopefully, you're now aware that these include neglecting to consult with an attorney when drafting or reviewing contracts. However, other mistakes you should be aware of include the following:

## Signing a contract you don't understand

Lack of understanding with regard to contracts doesn't just involve, as discussed previously, not comprehending the terminology. Frequently, it also involves not understanding the language at all. Commonly, for instance, when English isn't someone's first language, he or she signs contracts without thoroughly understanding what the contract obligates them to. If this is the case, I would advise you to seek an attorney that speaks your native language, or have the contract properly translated by a qualified interpreter.

## Blindly trusting the person you're entering into contract with

Often I see contracts that contain provisions unfavorable to my clients. However, when I point this out, the client tells me that the other party has assured them that it "does not plan to enforce that provision." In a commercial lease, for example, there may be a provision stating that the tenant must pay certain fees, but the prospective tenant is unconcerned because the landlord has verbally assured him that he "really never charges for that." Remember, a contract says what it says. It doesn't matter what the other party says verbally.

## Failing to negotiate terms that don't serve you

When considering entering into contract with a party who's drafted a contract that includes terms you aren't fully on board with, it is in your interests to negotiate those terms. In essence, the process of developing a contract is a negotiation unto itself. Each party's objective is to achieve what it needs and wants in an agreement that's beneficial for both. So when negotiating terms in a contract, don't just look at the terms you want to change—look at all of them. This will help you figure out which ones the other parties might be willing to negotiate. If, for example, you want a lower price on a product, the supplier you're contracting with might be willing to provide it if you allow longer delivery time or can be flexible regarding dates of delivery.

# Using a standard online contract without refining it to suit your unique business needs

As noted in chapter 2, there are many quite adequate contracts available online, and there is nothing wrong with using these—as long as you have an attorney customize them to your specific needs, as well as to any state and local requirements.

## Neglecting to include a termination clause

In chapter 6, we discussed including an exit clause in a partnership agreement. A termination clause is a similar provision. Business owners have many contractual relationships, not only with their partners in the business but also with suppliers and employees. Contracts shouldn't just provide for termination in the event of breach. They should include a way out for everyone involved, whenever it makes sense to do so. Say for instance you find a supplier who offers a better rate on a product or can perform a service more quickly. A termination clause will enable you to leave your present contractual relationship and enter a new one that's more to your benefit.

## Failing to specify the parties' obligations in the agreement

As discussed previously, a breach of contract is essentially a failure to perform the obligations specified in the contract. Another mistake small business owners make, however, is not being specific enough when they outline those obligations or how they're to be performed. It's usually clear, for instance, to establish breach should a contracted party fail to pay an amount they're obligated to. A business owner who fails to pay rent to a landlord with whom he's contracted to lease space is clearly not performing according to the obligations in the contract.

Other obligations, however, may be more subjective and thus less easy to prove in a breach case if not specified. A contract might, for instance, state that a social media marketer must produce and distribute a certain volume of content to advertise your business each month. If that content is inaccurate, unclear, uncompelling, and/or is not adequately distributed, however, you may wish to allege breach of contract. If the details of performance are outlined specifically in the contract, your case is more likely to succeed. Make sure, therefore, to define the performance requirements of each party you enter into contract with. In this example, for instance, you might specify how many clicks the content must receive, how many followers it must attract, and which social media it is to be posted on, etc.

## Entering into a poorly written contract

A poorly written contract can be as damaging to your business as no contract at all. Ambiguity, for example, either of the contract's terms or as created by superfluous language, can create confusion and lead to misunderstandings. Omission of important dates or other details can also lead to issues.

## Neglecting to include litigation provisions

Business contracts should always include a provision addressing how disputes are to be handled between contractual parties. As noted previously, for example, you may wish to specify that a mediation conference is required before resorting to litigation. Litigation provisions should also include whether a party found to have breached a contract will be liable for the costs of the dispute, stipulating, for instance, who is responsible for paying mediation, arbitration, or court costs and/or attorney's fees.

Contracts don't have to be complex. They should be simple. In fact, the simpler they are, the better. However, you need a basic understanding of what they are and how they work to safely enter into one.

In our next and final chapter, we'll take a look at our last mistake: staying in or initiating a lawsuit based on principle (a truly unwise and potentially costly idea).

## MISTAKE 8

# INITIATING OR STAYING IN A BUSINESS LAWSUIT ON THE BASIS OF PRINCIPLE

A while ago, I had a client who sold his share of the business to his then partner. A few years after purchasing it, however, the former partner decided he wasn't satisfied with what he had received, and he sued. His motivation wasn't only his dissatisfaction with his purchase, however. He also held a personal dislike for my client, an antipathy that continued to fuel the litigation far beyond what was necessary. Naturally, this upset my client, and a mutual hatred developed between the two parties, escalating to the point that it prolonged the litigation. The case went on for so long that both parties' resources were eventually totally depleted.

This business lawsuit was not solely about money; it was also about "principle." In other words, the parties were so emotional that they were willing to lose everything to try to prove the other "wrong."

As this example illustrates, either initiating or staying in a business lawsuit on the basis of principle can be a time-consuming, costly, and often futile endeavor.

This is true for many reasons:

- Business lawsuits are not about proving principles.

- Lawsuits take a lot of time to decide.

- Lawsuits are expensive.

- Even if you win a lawsuit, you might not be able to collect money.

# Business Lawsuits are Not about Proving Principles

But wait, you might be thinking: Isn't the law intended to prove who's right and who's wrong? If I know I'm right, why shouldn't I try to prove it?

Well, the reality is that business lawsuits aren't really about proving principles. A business lawsuit's function is not to enforce morality. The goal isn't to prove the way things "should" or "should not" be. Instead, it's simply to determine the degree of monetary damages, if any, you've suffered and to decide what financial compensation you may be legally entitled to. In other words, to make you "whole."

# Lawsuits Take a Lot of Time to Decide

Additionally, even if you have a strong basis for bringing a lawsuit against someone you can prove has wronged you, taking a lawsuit to trial takes a great deal of time. The median time from filing to disposition in civil cases is almost nine months, and from filing to trial, it's almost two years!

# Lawsuits Are Expensive

Further, lawsuits are expensive. The Small Business Administration (SBA) reports that costs for litigation generally range from $3,000 to $150,000, with approximately one-third of cases costing under $10,000,[8] figures that are likely even higher now than when initially reported.

Why are lawsuits so expensive? Well, because they take so long and involve so much preparation. As noted, it usually takes about two years to take a case from inception to trial. For the first year and a half of that time, most of the legal work attorneys do is spent in what we call "motion practice" and "discovery." Motions are when we ask the judge to rule on something in your favor, and discovery is gathering evidence for trial. For instance, if the opposing side is not cooperating (which happens often), or if there is a dispute regarding the type of documents that should be produced, an attorney can file a motion to dismiss the lawsuit or a motion to compel discovery and schedule the matter for hearing. The preparation of these motions and appearances in court is time consuming and a drain on financial resources. Also, during the discovery process, we attorneys are reviewing documents, taking depositions (witnesses' sworn out-of-court testimony), and liti-

---

8    Klemm Analysis Group, "Impact of Litigation on Small Business," Small Business Administration Office of Advocacy, no. 265 (October 2005): 1, https://www.sba.gov/sites/default/files/files/rs265tot.pdf.

gating discovery disputes with the opposing attorney. Your attorney will likely charge you on an hourly basis for the time it takes to do all this, and you will also be paying for his or her staff's time (for paralegals to do research, for example).

Further, when you bring a lawsuit, you are entering into an adversarial system in which there will be a "winner" and a "loser," meaning that not only are you fighting for what you want, but you are fighting against the opposing attorney, the process of which can be financially devastating. During a discovery, for instance, the opposing attorney may serve you with interrogatories (written questions about details relevant to the case), as well as requests for production of documents and/or requests for admissions (written statements in which you admit or deny certain key facts). Your attorney will have to prepare responses for all such requests, and even though you didn't initiate them, you will be responsible for paying for them.

In the adversarial system, therefore, lawsuits are not only about winning cases; they are also about battles of resources and skills—your attorney's skills versus those of the opposing attorney. You're in a fight to see whose resources will last the longest, and you're also gambling on your attorney's ability to gather information, present the case, and spar with the opposing attorney.

**THE COSTS OF LITIGATION CAN EXTEND FAR BEYOND YOUR TIME AND POCKETBOOK.**

Consider, too, that this is all just in *preparation* for a trial that may never even happen. The vast majority of civil cases are resolved by means other than a trial. Further, in addition to your attorney's fees, if you do go to trial, you will have to pay outside vendors, such as court reporters, process servers, couriers, and others who provide services for your case—not to mention the possibility of appeals, which will cost you more money still.

The costs of litigation can extend far beyond your time and pocketbook. The SBA also reports that the impact of litigation on small businesses is not limited to the financial expense of legal fees. Because most small business owners are personally invested in their businesses, litigation can cause not only monetary loss but also significant emotional stress, which may affect how business is conducted. Due to its high cost, for instance, many small business owners who undergo litigation feel they need to compensate for their losses. Because raising prices would put them at a competitive disadvantage, however, they're necessitated to do this by reducing operating expenses, expanding their customer base, and/or adding services.[9]

I caution all my clients to think about the expense of a lawsuit, and when it comes to the subject of suing on the basis of principle, I can't emphasize this caution enough. Because once you pull the "lawsuit trigger," it's like an open checkbook with no end in sight.

## Even If You Win a Lawsuit, You Might Not Be Able to Collect Money

Still, if you win your case, you stand to recoup your expenses and more, right? Not necessarily. Winning a case doesn't mean you automatically receive money. If the entity you're suing is bankrupt or just doesn't pay, you may have to start another legal procedure against them, in bankruptcy court, to try to collect, adding more time and expense to those costs you've already accumulated.

Finally, to add insult to injury, even if you win your case, you won't necessarily receive legal fees as part of whatever damages the court determines you're entitled to.

---

9    Ibid.

# Questions to Ask Yourself before Deciding to Sue

For these reasons, it's important to ask yourself several of the questions that follow before you decide whether to file a lawsuit:

- Why am I suing?

- Who am I suing?

- Where is the entity I am suing located?

- What do I want to gain from this lawsuit?

- What is this going to cost me?

- How long will this take?

- How much am I willing to settle for?

- What is the cost of doing nothing?

- How much am I willing to lose?

- Is there anything else I would rather use this money for?

Let's review these questions in more detail:

## Why am I suing?

Why you're suing is one of the most important questions you need to answer before initiating a lawsuit. If you're suing in a civil court for a business-related matter, the answer should be "For money." Again, I'm not saying that whatever principle may be relevant to the matter isn't justified. I'm just saying that in the context of a business dispute, the reason to sue is money, not principle. Usually, as a small business owner, you will be suing over loss of money that was legally owed to you.

## Who am I suing?

It's not always as clear as you might think who the defendant in a lawsuit is. You might believe you need to sue an individual, for instance, when in fact, you need to sue a corporation, or vice versa. Your attorney will, therefore, need to make that evaluation.

## Where is the entity I am suing located?

In addition to determining who the defendant is, your attorney will also need to verify the location of the entity you're suing. Some businesses, for example, have a presence in one state but are incorporated in another. This is often the situation in cases in which real estate is involved. A small business owner leasing space in a building, for instance, might try to sue the property manager of that building, rather than the landlord, who's located in another state. Since the property manager doesn't own the building, the business owner in such a situation would be filing the lawsuit in vain.

## What is this going to cost me?

As we've discussed, lawsuits are expensive. So you have to decide how much you're going to spend to try to recover what you believe you have lost. There's little point in spending as much (or even almost as much, given the time it will also cost you) as what you may stand to gain. Consequently, again, it's advisable to set aside any matters of principle you may feel justify a lawsuit and answer this question solely from a business perspective.

This caution might be difficult to abide by. You might feel betrayed or ignored or resentful and want to pursue a case to vindicate a wrong. However, you have to look at the prospect of launching a lawsuit as you would a calculated gamble. You're making a decision as to whether to invest good money after bad. Is it worth the risk? There's no such thing as a "slam dunk" case. You might think you're sure to win, but the defendant will always come up with defenses (defenses that are costly to respond to) to your allegations.

The point is that, if you're considering suing someone, it's important to have an honest conversation with your attorney about the expected cost of litigation because the costs involve much more than just going to trial. Behind the scenes there are hundreds of emails that must be answered, requests from opposing attorneys that must be responded to, as well as witnesses who must be located, go through depositions, and testify. A two-hour deposition involving a court reporter and generating a transcript can cost around $800. Multiply that by ten witnesses, and this part of the discovery process alone can cost $8,000.

These are just some of the costs that can be roughly predicted. They don't include those expenses generated by the opposing attorney. Such expenses are essentially a wild card because business litigation is about capitalizing on the mistakes of the other attorney. In other words, your attorney is challenged in at least two different ways: he or she must not only gather the facts from you and from the opposing side but must also sidestep, or recover from, the opposing attorney's attempts to legally undermine the advancement of your case.

One analogy I like to use to bring home this point is to compare the process of a lawsuit to what sometimes, regrettably, occurs when you hire a contractor to renovate your house. The contractor arrives at your property, sets up his equipment, and lays out the supplies you've already paid for in preparation to begin work the next day. Overnight, however, someone steals them all away, leaving you with nothing but a hole in your pocket. Bringing a lawsuit is something like that. New facts come to light, and then the opposing attorney comes in and uses procedure as a sword to put psychological pressure on your attorney and on you to spend more money to address them. This is all fair game in business litigation.

Long story short, you can be unequivocally right in your claim against someone and still lose your case by spending more than it's worth to "win." So you have to break down all costs, not just your attorney's fees, and perform a realistic cost-benefit analysis before making a decision as to whether to sue.

## How long will it take?

As mentioned, lawsuits take about two years to resolve. This might not sound like a long time, but on a daily basis, it can feel like much longer and take a significant toll on your well-being. Think about the emotional ups and downs, the time away from work, the constant stress of the uncertainty and financial costs, the wear and tear it may take on your personal and professional relationships. Time only flies when you're having fun, not so much when you're involved in a lawsuit.

## How much am I willing to settle for?

The earlier you decide how much you're willing to settle for, the less money you'll spend on legal fees. So if you're willing to settle a lawsuit without going to court, you're already ahead of the game. For one thing, you'll be settling the dispute without risking having the other party sue you in return. For another, by choosing to settle, you have much greater control over the dispute's resolution and your costs. One of the quotations I like to share with my clients comes from a judge who, while discussing settlement during mediation, said that when you settle, "you have control, you have certainty, and you have closure."

## What is the cost of doing nothing?

If you're the party who's suing, you will also want to consider what the cost of doing nothing at all is as compared with initiating a process that's going to be emotionally and financially draining. Remember, there's a lot more to lose in addition to the money you may be able to collect if you win your suit. It may be less expensive to simply swallow your losses and move on.

This of course is an individual decision; however, asking yourself if you can afford the expense of, say, $10,000 to attempt to win and possibly collect $20,000 isn't one to be overlooked. Many business owners work on very limited budgets, so paying for the costs of bringing a lawsuit may necessitate using credit cards, savings, or cashing in investments. Knowing where you will find the funds for litigation and whether you can afford to risk them is important. If you find that you either can't afford it or can only barely afford it, it's better not to even start it. If you do, the expenses will surpass your predictions, and you will end up losing more money than you already have.

## How much am I willing to lose?

Like many of the other questions you'll need to ask yourself in the process of determining whether to initiate or stay in a lawsuit, this one has no right or wrong answer but is instead an individual choice. Deciding how much you are willing to lose is a question based on how much risk you are willing to undertake. You may, for instance, after speaking with your attorney, have a rough estimate of how much you expect bringing a lawsuit to cost. However, you should also be aware that, should you lose, you could also end up paying the other side's attorney fees. Again, there's a lot more to lose in addition to the money you pay up front to try to collect.

## Is there anything else I would rather use this money for?

Very few business owners have a fund set aside for lawsuits. That's what insurance is for. So the money you're considering investing in a lawsuit is, most likely, money that's earmarked for something else, or money that could be invested, either back into the business (potentially earning you back the money you've lost) or for your own personal use. Consequently, you'll need to pay yourself back by generating additional revenue, a possibility that may or may not be feasible but that will cost you time and more expense at a time when you already have less working capital, potentially putting a strain on your business.

There are no right or wrong answers to any of these questions. However, only after carefully answering all of them can you *begin* to make an informed and rational decision as to whether to initiate a lawsuit.

# Analyzing the Strength of Your Case

*Begin* to make a decision? That is correct. Answering the aforementioned questions is just the start of an analysis as to whether to initiate or stay in a lawsuit. The next stage is to analyze the strength of your case.

Analyzing the strength of your case includes several steps: First, you will need to establish a timeline, a chronology of events that ascertains (for example, in a breach of contract) when the contract began, what the event was that you contend created its breach, and what damages you suffered as a result. Second, you have to identify what events took place as a result of the alleged breach. Third, you have to gather documentation to support your contention that these events caused damage: Are there written records of losses? Do you have witnesses? If so, can they be located? Are you on good terms with them? Do they speak English? (If not, you will need to pay certified translation fees.) If, for example, your chief witness is a former employee who doesn't speak English and who now lives in South America, it may prove logistically challenging to rely on that witness.

# What to Do When You Are Being Sued

If you yourself are being sued by someone else, you have no choice but to defend yourself.

Sometimes, clients who've been sued come to me saying that they want to counterclaim. A counterclaim, however, involves twice the work of a lawsuit. This is because not only must you defend yourself, but you're also suing the other party. A counterclaim entails going through the same analysis as described previously, such as asking how much it will cost, whether you can afford it, and whether you have a strong case.

It is therefore often much less expensive to avoid a counterclaim (especially one that, it hopefully by now goes without saying, is based on principle). Instead, when you find yourself in the position of defending yourself in a lawsuit, your game plan should be to reduce the risk and minimize your financial exposure, either by negotiated settlement or via strategic litigation.

You might, for instance, consider that sometimes, in the interests of saving their own time and money, the party suing you will accept a smaller amount than the figure for which they are asking. If the other party is asking for $30,000, they are likely to pay at least $10,000 to bring the case to trial, bringing the amount they stand to gain to $20,000. If you then negotiate to settle for half of that, the other party may view this as preferable to the strain and gamble of going to court. While negotiating a $10,000 settlement may still be a difficult pill to swallow, it is likely in your interests to consider the compromise.

If, on the other hand, the amount in question is much higher, say, a million or more, strategic litigation may be a better course of action. What I mean by strategic litigation is using legal tools to negotiate a better outcome.

You could, for instance, raise valid defenses to push the other side to gather the information they need to make their case. Your attorney's requests for the plaintiff's interrogatories, documents, and admissions, for example, are legitimate. However, as discussed, they also serve to tax the plaintiff's financial and emotional resources.

Using strategic litigation tools and tactics impresses upon the plaintiff the reality of what he or she is up against. If, for instance, your attorney requests a deposition of the plaintiff, nine out of ten times, the plaintiff will find that deposition quite unpleasant. Depositions can be intrusive, exposing the personal details of people's lives and putting them in a defensive and vulnerable position. Most people find them highly objectionable and prefer to avoid them. Once having experienced the litigation process, though, they may be much more willing to settle out of court.

# Alternatives to Filing a Lawsuit

If, after conducting a thorough cost-benefit and case analysis, you decide you have a strong case that's not based on principle, and you want to go ahead with filing a lawsuit or counterclaim, it is nonetheless always a good idea to consider alternatives to battling it out in court.

Court cases are not only time consuming, expensive, and unpredictable in terms of collecting damages, but they also limit the amount of control you have as to the outcome. In a court case, you are handing over the decision to a judge and jury. Once you've done that, the matter is effectively out of your hands; you have no idea who the judge or jurors will be, how they think, or whether they will rule in your favor.

In other forms of dispute resolution, however, such as mediation, you have more agency. I like to share with my clients what I learned from another mediator as the "Eight C's" of the alternative dispute resolution process: client control, cost control, comfort, commitment, courtesy, creativity, confidentiality, and compromise.

## Client Control

As discussed, when you litigate a dispute in a courtroom, you are essentially asking a judge and jury to resolve the problem for you. Therefore, you relinquish considerable control over the resulting decision. If you enter mediation to settle a dispute, however, you have more control in the decision-making process because all parties participate in the discussion and resolve the issue together. Further, in mediation, you may have more control over the time in which it takes to reach a decision, because it may be possible to reach a solution more quickly than you would in court.

## Cost Control

Similarly, in a mediation, you may have more control over costs. This is because, rather than having to pay both your own attorney's costs and those expenses generated by the opposing attorney in the course of discovery, you may be able to negotiate a damages amount that's acceptable to you before you agree to a settlement. The ability to arrive at a resolution more quickly than may be possible in court may also save you money.

# Comfort

Mediation doesn't take place in a courtroom, sitting on uncomfortable benches while facing a judge and jury and wondering how your case is going to end. Instead, it's an informal process that involves a series of conversations with a trained and impartial third-party mediator in the privacy of his or her offices or via video conference. The mediator has no power to render a decision regarding the dispute but is merely a neutral facilitator of the discussion. The more comfortable environment, the ability to participate in the discussions rather than simply awaiting a jury verdict, and the fact that the process is not confrontational but cooperative all contribute to making the mediation process far more comfortable than litigation.

# Commitment

Mediators often aim to keep parties in dispute in the mediation process until the dispute is settled or at an impasse. This means that both sides need to commit to the process, and since committing to finding a solution is a more collaborative than combative approach to resolving a dispute, it tends to lower the emotional temperature, enabling both sides to act more reasonably.

# Courtesy

Mediation does not involve one party trying to win at the expense of another. Instead, it strives to achieve "win-win" solutions for both parties, a goal that necessitates courteous behavior on both sides. Working together to find a solution that satisfies each party, perhaps not fully but at least sufficiently, is often palatable, especially because compromises in terms of settlement amounts are offset by saving time and money that would otherwise be spent in litigation.

## Creativity

Unlike in a courtroom setting, in which a judge and jury have set procedures and processes for deciding a case, mediation offers the opportunity to be creative in terms of solutions. In a courtroom, there will be a winner and a loser, and the verdict will be monetary. Mediation, however, enables creative compromises and possible "win-win" solutions that may or may not be solely monetary.

## Confidentiality

For the most part, mediation proceedings are confidential. Rather than having the dispute be on the public record, as it is when you litigate in court, mediation provides a way to keep it relatively private. This is often preferable when personal or sensitive information is involved.

## Compromise

In mediation, there are no winners or losers. Both sides walk away having compromised. This has many benefits for both parties, one of which is the potential to minimize adversarial attitudes and avoid the hard feelings that often result from litigation. Keeping relationships with the people with whom you are in dispute free of rancor may sometimes serve your business and/or personal interests.

> THE MEDIATION PROCESS IS USUALLY A HIGHLY SATISFACTORY WAY TO ADDRESS MANY SMALL BUSINESS DISPUTES.

I personally often recommend mediation to my clients. If you have an attorney who understands your rights, knows what your case is worth, and is dedicated to working on your behalf, the mediation process is usually a highly satisfactory way to address many small business disputes.

# A Few Final Words

One of the most common situations in which I see small business owners becoming involved in lawsuits based on principle is when they have both a personal (particularly a romantic) and a business relationship. When there is a dispute between such business owners, it tends to create an emotionally charged environment that tempts them to sue each other based on their feelings or on "principles" they want to prove.

As is, I hope, now clear, this is a bad idea. In some cases, such business owners share joint bank accounts and mutually own properties, making any disagreements that escalate to the level of litigation much more complicated to resolve. Rather than being able to deal with the dispute in an arm's-length fashion, with the parties' attorneys conducting most of the interactions for them, these cases can become embroiled in arguments about issues that have nothing to do with the business.

When this happens, it's likely to necessitate that attorneys not only assist with the case's legal aspects but also act as counselors in an attempt to encourage the parties to move on. Intent on "punishing" each other, however, the parties in these cases can continue to litigate for a very long time, costing themselves a great deal of time, distress, and money.

Needless to say, such emotionally contentious "business" disputes should be avoided. However, whether you are in such a relationship or not, and regardless of whether you are a plaintiff or a defendant, a lawsuit will be a drain on your time, as well as on your financial and emotional resources.

Very seldom does anyone have the financial ability to take a case all the way to trial, and those who do usually know better. It's wise, therefore, to think carefully about all the questions this chapter outlines, discuss them honestly and thoroughly with your attorney, and clearly communicate your goals. If after having done so you still want to proceed, that's your choice. At the very minimum, regardless of what you decide, you will at least know that, rather than making a choice based on principle, you have given this very important decision serious thought.

# CLOSING ARGUMENTS

Hopefully, now that you've read this book, it's clear that hiring an attorney to help you with your small business concerns is likely a good idea. Many of the clients I meet get themselves into difficult situations after taking a DIY approach to legal problems, digging themselves into even deeper holes. Often, these situations could have been avoided had they simply consulted an attorney prior to starting their business, or at least, at the first sign of trouble.

Everything we do involves risk. It's unnecessary, though, to take more risks than can be prevented with a few precautionary measures, and although consulting with an attorney can't protect you from ever facing a lawsuit, it can go a long way toward decreasing the likelihood of a dispute or a potential claim.

As a business owner, you need a team of people to help your business be successful. My firm's slogan, "Our Goal Is to Help You Succeed," acknowledges this, and it is my personal and professional commitment to my clients. I see myself as my clients' legal business partner: my job is to protect them from legal challenges as much as possible and to solve those legal problems that do arise quickly and efficiently.

I truly appreciate the time you've taken to read this book, and I hope that it has provided you with some useful insights and information that you can apply to your business.

Good luck in your journey!

*Rich Sierra*

# ABOUT RICH SIERRA

Rich Sierra is the founder and CEO of Florida Small Business Legal Center and has counseled thousands of business owners since 2004. The firm continues to grow at a rapid pace, with his main office in Boca Raton, Florida, and satellite offices in Miami, Weston, Coconut Creek, and Orlando. The key to the success of his practice is an innovative marketing system and a high level of efficiency in the delivery of cost-effective legal services.

Florida Small Business Legal Center focuses exclusively on providing legal services to the business community and individuals with business-related issues. The cases that the firm has handled include breach of contract litigation, franchise disputes, shareholder disputes, partnership disputes, representing buyers or sellers in the purchase or sale of a business, serving as in-house counsel for businesses, real estate litigation, review of commercial leases, and many other legal matters that affect the business owner.

The firm's client base is just as diverse as the businesses community it serves. He represents martial art studios, pizza franchises and other restaurants, international distributors and manufacturers of women's hair products, medical equipment sales, software consultants, nutritional supplement manufacturers, professional coffee-equipment repair services and distributors, independent consultants, and many others. Although most of the firm's clients are in South Florida, it also represents clients from Europe and the Middle East.

Before opening his law practice, Rich Sierra was the founder and CEO of Healthcare Recruitment Online, a national job board for healthcare professionals. He ran the company for eight years before it was acquired in 2004 by another organization. His experience as an entrepreneur of a national online company gave him the experience to understand the many legal issues that business owners face in running their businesses. Also, it allowed him to fine-tune his marketing skills, skills that he has since applied successfully to his law practice. He is frequently asked to speak to other attorneys about marketing strategies for law firms; he was a contributor to AVVO's *Lawyernomics* blog, and he has been an AVVO Top-Rated Lawyer for several years, as well as being a member of Lawyers of Distinction since 2021.

Rich Sierra earned a BS degree in marketing from the University of Tampa and a JD degree from Nova Southeastern University Law Center in Fort Lauderdale. In addition to being admitted to the Florida Bar, he is also admitted to the United States District Court Southern and Middle Districts of Florida.

Rich lives with his lovely wife, Sharon, and his family in Parkland, Florida, where they are avid practitioners of martial arts. Rich and Sharon have black belts in tae kwon do, and Rich also has a black belt in judo and a purple belt in Brazilian jiujitsu. They enjoy traveling, concerts, and visiting Vegas, which is their favorite city!

# ACKNOWLEDGEMENTS

This book has been over ten years in the making and it has gone through several revisions as I gained more experience as a business lawyer and was exposed to more legal issues affecting my clients. I would like to thank the staff of Advantage Media and Forbes Books for the invitation to become a featured author. I am very glad that I accepted the challenge, and it has been an opportunity for growth for me. I'd also like to thank my clients that for the last eighteen years have trusted me to handle their business legal issues and inspired me to write this book; the staff from the Florida Small Business Legal Center, especially Aimee Carlin, who for the last thirteen years has been instrumental in the growth of the practice; to my family, Michael, Caroline, Jonathan, and Max  and my brothers, Jose and Dennis, for their unwavering support and encouragement in pursuing this project, and last but not least, my gorgeous wife Sharon who came up with the idea of the title of the book and has listened to countless of hours of me discussing ideas and topics for the book. Love you baby!